U.S.–Canadian
Economic Relations

Brookings Dialogues on Public Policy

*The presentations and discussions at Brookings conferences and seminars
often deserve wide circulation as contributions to public understanding
of issues of national importance. The Brookings Dialogues on Public
Policy series is intended to make such statements and commentary
available to a broad and general audience, usually in summary form.
The series supplements the Institution's research publications by
reflecting the contrasting, often lively, and sometimes conflicting views of
elected and appointed government officials, other leaders in public and
private life, and scholars. In keeping with their origin and purpose, the
Dialogues are not subjected to the formal review procedures established
for the Institution's research publications. Brookings publishes them
in the belief that they are worthy of public consideration but does
not assume responsibility for their accuracy or objectivity. And, as
in all Brookings publications, the judgments, conclusions, and
recommendations presented in the Dialogues should not be ascribed to the
trustees, officers, or other staff members of the Brookings Institution.*

U.S.-Canadian Economic Relations
Next Steps?

Papers by   MITCHELL SHARP

GEORGE W. BALL

SIMON S. REISMAN

MYER RASHISH

WILLIAM E. BROCK

ROWLAND C. FRAZEE

HUGH P. DONAGHUE

JAMES R. SCHLESINGER

MARSHALL A. CROWE

ALLAN E. GOTLIEB

*presented at a conference at the Brookings Institution
chaired by Bruce K. MacLaury on April 10, 1984*

Edited by   EDWARD R. FRIED *and* PHILIP H. TREZISE

THE BROOKINGS INSTITUTION
Washington, D.C.

About Brookings

THE BROOKINGS INSTITUTION is a private nonprofit organization devoted to research, education, and publication in economics, government, foreign policy, and the social sciences generally. Its principal purpose is to bring knowledge to bear on the current and emerging public policy problems facing the American people. In its research, Brookings functions as an independent analyst and critic, committed to publishing its findings for the information of the public. In its conferences and other activities, it serves as a bridge between scholarship and public policy, bringing new knowledge to the attention of decisionmakers and affording scholars a better insight into policy issues. Its activities are carried out through three research programs (Economic Studies, Governmental Studies, Foreign Policy Studies), an Advanced Study Program, a Publications Program, and a Social Science Computation Center.

The Institution was incorporated in 1927 to merge the Institute for Government Research, founded in 1916 as the first private organization devoted to public policy issues at the national level; the Institute of Economics, established in 1922 to study economic problems; and the Robert Brookings Graduate School of Economics and Government, organized in 1924 as a pioneering experiment in training for public service. The consolidated institution was named in honor of Robert Somers Brookings (1850–1932), a St. Louis businessman whose leadership shaped the earlier organizations.

Brookings is financed largely by endowment and by the support of philanthropic foundations, corporations, and private individuals. Its funds are devoted to carrying out its own research and educational activities. It also undertakes some unclassified government contract studies, reserving the right to publish its findings.

A Board of Trustees is responsible for general supervision of the Institution, approval of fields of investigation, and safeguarding the independence of the Institution's work. The President is the chief administrative officer, responsible for formulating and coordinating policies, recommending projects, approving publications, and selecting the staff.

Preface

CANADIANS commonly complain that Americans take Canada for granted. If there is basis for the complaint, the principal reason doubtless is the generally even tenor of Canadian-American relations, which is itself one of the more agreeable and durable facts of international life. Excitement is most readily generated when good relations are not automatically assumed. But, of course, the United States can never really be indifferent to a neighbor with whom it is so closely linked by geography, politics, and economics.

Trade is a major force tying the two countries together. Its dimensions are not always well understood. Last year the value of U.S. two-way merchandise trade with Canada exceeded that with all ten countries of the European Community. It was 43 percent greater than trade with Japan. For Canada, trade with the United States was 72 percent of total foreign trade. All trading sectors are represented, led by manufactures. Few regions in either country can be untouched by this rewarding exchange.

The pages that follow record the proceedings of a conference in which distinguished Canadians and Americans—businessmen and present and former government officials—gave their views on the bilateral economic relationship. The emphasis was on trade and, more specifically, on the possibilities for the removal of barriers to its further growth, ranging from new bilateral sectoral free-trade arrangements to a full free-trade area. The discussion brought out not only the expected range of opinions but a number of new approaches to bilateral trade policies and the politics surrounding them.

The Brookings Institution is pleased to publish this latest volume in its Dialogues on Public Policy series. We are grateful to the Canadian Embassy and the William H. Donner Foundation, Inc. for providing support to help finance the conference and the publication.

vii

The editors are indebted to Barbara Littell and Julia Sternberg of the Brookings Advanced Study Program, who managed the organizational arrangements for the conference; to James Schneider, who prepared the manuscript for publication; and to Janet Smith for typing successive versions of the text.

BRUCE K. MAC LAURY
President

September 1984
Washington, D.C.

Contents

An Introductory Perspective

EDWARD R. FRIED *and* PHILIP H. TREZISE

That long frontier from the Atlantic to the Pacific oceans, guarded only by neighborly respect and honorable obligations, is an example to every country and a pattern for the future of the world.
Winston Churchill, April 20, 1939

CHURCHILL's rolling prose expresses a well-remarked feature of the relationship between the United States and Canada. The two nations have lived at peace and in harmony to an extent that is unusual and exemplary. Nobody imagines that this situation could change. Amity between these North American neighbors is considered fundamental and enduring.

Of course, even the most congenial neighbors will have differences of opinion and, sometimes, of interest; Canada and the United States are no exception. Issues do arise and, in accord with tradition and long practice, are negotiated and resolved, though not always as swiftly or as adequately as one or the other of the parties would wish. Most of these issues derive initially from transborder economic relations, which are as extensive as the border is long. This volume of proceedings of a conference on relations between Canada and the United States accordingly has as its focus bilateral economic affairs and their inevitable political implications.

If there is a theme common to the several conference papers, it can be put as a question: Are Canada and the United States making the most of their joint occupancy of a rich continent? Or, put another way, supposing that the frontier was not only unguarded but was also open freely to the exchange of goods and services, would not both peoples be better off?

In fact, the idea of a North American free-trade area is older than the Canadian confederation. Simon Reisman's essay in this volume, which presents the case for full free trade in goods and services coupled with national treatment for investment, begins with an absorbing account of Canadian policy toward trade with the United States from the Reciprocity Treaty of 1854 onward. Recurrently, as he points out, Canadian political leaders have been

I

drawn to the thought of a far-reaching trade arrangement with the United States. But because the American responses were cool or negative and for domestic reasons as well, the main line of Canadian policy through World War II was protectionism with respect to the United States and preferences for the United Kingdom.

The trade policy of the United States over the same years was generally protectionist against all nations, culminating in the indiscriminately high duties written into the Tariff Act of 1930. The reaction to this unfortunate piece of legislation came in the Trade Agreements Act of 1934, which marked the entry of modern American trade policy centered on trade liberalization, and the beginning of a joint and gradual dismantling of barriers to trade with Canada. Geography, resources, and affluence work strongly to pull the two economies together. Thus, and perhaps especially now when the multilateral trading order has come under severe strain, it is not surprising that Canadians and Americans would be looking again at the possibilities for mutual benefit from an agreement to remove the artificial barriers to trade that are still found on both sides of their common border.

That barriers do remain is testimony, however, to powerful contrary impulses. Free trade, even bilateral free trade, is far from being seen by everyone as a unmixed good. In both Canada and the United States the status quo in trade policy has numerous and influential supporters. Any proposal to widen the existing scope of unrestricted Canadian-U.S. trade will infallibly attract opposition from some of the interests likely to be affected. Where protection exists, somebody enjoys an official grant of at least partial relief from foreign competition. Few of the beneficiaries will be prepared readily to forgo the favor.

These obstacles are well understood. Strong as they are, however, they have not prevented the post–World War II march toward removing trade barriers. Net gains from trade, which have been evident and large, have proved to be the overriding force.

In Canada, objections from specific economic sectors will be reinforced by a more general concern about the consequences of free trade for the national identity and political independence. Mitchell Sharp dramatizes the breadth of this concern by pointing out in his paper that no elected member of Parliament has supported the idea of a free-trade area with the United States. To many Canadians a formal economic partnership with the United States, which has ten times Canada's population and a gross national product more than eleven times as large, appears an inherent threat to the idea of a separate Canada. George Ball recalls later in this volume the hostile Canadian reaction to his 1968 suggestion that commercial imperatives would in time bring substantial economic integration with the United States and a measure of common political decisionmaking as well. That prospect, at least for a number of vocal Canadians, was anything but desirable. Their point of view may well be the most formidable obstacle of any in either country to a new effort to remove all or most of the remaining restrictions on the exchange of goods and services.

The asymmetry in the gross numbers is immutably there. Canada's population is 25 million, that of the United States 235 million. Still, that is not the whole picture. From another perspective, Canada looks less vulnerable and more like an extremely vigorous partner in the economic relationship with the United States.

In both countries it is commonly and wrongly believed that Canada is primarily an exporter of raw materials—natural resources. Actually, Canadian exports to the United States are dominated by manufactured goods. In 1983, shipments of manufactures from Canada to the United States valued at $30.6 billion exceeded exports of American manufactured goods to Canada by $3.3 billion. Per capita, the differential was enormous. Canadians on average produced $1,200 worth of manufactures to be sold in the United States. The comparable figure for the United States was one-tenth as large, $118.

When the bilateral trade account is viewed in total, this disparity widens, reflecting the sizable overall Canadian surplus. In 1983, Canadian per capita exports to the United States of goods of all kinds were valued at $2,200, while Americans exported goods worth $160 to Canada.

When the perspective is in relative rather than absolute terms, Canada is also the more active partner in direct investment. To be sure, the volume of U.S. direct investment in Canada ($45 billion in 1982) looms large in Canadian industry, while Canadian direct investment in the United States ($9 billion in 1982) is a small fraction of U.S. industry. Per capita, however, Canadians have invested almost twice as much in the United States as Americans have in Canada ($368 as against $196 in 1982).

These considerations obviously are not likely to alter matters if most Canadians indeed see a closer economic association with the United States as endangering Canada's independence. At the same time, the importance for Canadian incomes of trade and investment relations with the United States, the attraction of a more open American market, and a desire to be insulated from possible U.S. restrictionist actions seem bound to keep alive in Canada the thought of further advances toward bilateral free trade. Because U.S. trade interests are so wide, a free-trade agreement with Canada is naturally less exciting to Americans. There seems no compelling reason, however, to expect that such an agreement would be unacceptable to the Congress and the country. Ambassador Brock stated the position strongly in asserting that the U.S. administration would match Canadian government trade initiatives stride for stride and that Congress might be particularly receptive to a positive approach to trade—for a change.

A possible objection is to bilateralism as such. Bilateral trade arrangements, including bilateral arrangements by industrial sectors, typically will bring smaller efficiency gains than will freer trade over a wider area. Canada and the United States are committed, moreover, to the General Agreement on Tariffs and Trade (GATT) and its unconditional most-favored-nation, multilateral foundation. Neither should wish to weaken further an already battered charter and institution. But, as is pointed out elsewhere in this volume, compliance with the definition of free-trade areas in GATT Article 24 could be within range. The literal requirement is that tariffs and other restrictions be eliminated on substantially all the trade among the participants. On the precedent of the European Free Trade Association (EFTA), the goal of substantial elimination is one that may be reached over a prescribed period of time. If it is correctly estimated that 80 percent of exports from Canada will soon enter the United States duty free under existing agreements and that 65 percent of American sales to Canada are to be similarly treated, then the extension of free entry to a relatively few heavily traded products probably could satisfy the criterion of Article 24. The political problem presumably could then arise. Meeting GATT requirements for a free-trade area would symbolize at least that Canada had entered a new, closer, phase in its relations with the United States.

Strictly speaking, the bilateral free-trade outcome doubtless would be inferior for both Canada and the United States to a really significant move toward free or at least freer trade on a more nearly global basis. Realistically, however, the prospects for an early and general reduction of worldwide barriers to trade are not encouraging. Nor need a Canadian-U.S. agreement impede progress toward further multilateral negotiations for trade liberalization. It might serve to hasten another negotiating round.

Services may be a trade sector in which a North American initiative could break new ground. Because GATT is silent on the subject, relatively little has been done to establish rules or standards for trade in services. Now that advances in communications technology have broadened the field, the case has strengthened for an early try at reaching international agreement on the treatment to be accorded some of the services that have international markets. Papers by Rowland Frazee and Hugh Donaghue in this volume deal with the issue of computer data flows across national boundaries in the context of Canadian-American commercial and financial relations. A bilateral undertaking to avoid protectionist restrictions on these data flows would not raise GATT problems and might encourage consideration of a multilateral code along similar lines.

The gains from bilateral free trade supposedly would accrue in larger part to Canada. The argument usually advanced is that much of Canadian industry now operates below an optimum level because of the small size of the domestic market. Greater access to the United States would overcome this source of inefficiency for sectors and companies newly able to compete across the border. With its large domestic market American industry has less to gain. This reasoning is not implausible but neither is it altogether convincing. If not offset or hampered by other official measures, the removal of restrictions at the border inevitably will lead to some reshuffling of productive activity within the affected sectors and in due course beyond. Neoclassical economics tells us that the result will be to raise levels of efficiency for all concerned. Against these more or less lasting benefits must then be put the more immediate costs of adjustment. To attempt to measure and allocate in advance the net gains from this dynamic process is a questionable exercise. Theory and experience say that there should be higher incomes for Canadians and Americans alike. That proposition must be a principal justification for the effort.

Several speakers at the conference noted that the gains to be expected from eliminating traditional restrictions on trade could be diminished or nullified by greater resort to nontariff barriers. This point has force, as may be seen in the record of the largest of free-trade experiments, the European Community's customs union, where obstacles other than tariffs continue to hamper the flow of commerce among the ten member nations. It seems fair to say, however, that the problem is much less a reason to forgo action on tariffs than it is a challenge to negotiators to seek ways to minimize the potential impact of nontariff barriers. In his presentation, Myer Rashish argues that agreements between Canada and the United States to remove specific nontariff barriers would be the most fruitful bilateral approach to take at the present time.

Energy fuels are not usually thought of as falling within the scope of conventional trade policy. Given that the dominant fuel entering international trade is under the control and management of a producers' cartel, this is understandable. Nevertheless, fuels have an important and at times controversial role in Canadian-U.S. trade. Many of the controversies have occurred when either government or both have chosen to substitute official judgments for market forces through import restrictions or price controls. It cannot be said that these episodes have shown public authorities to have possessed unusual wisdom. The transborder energy trade, however, is now gradually but steadily becoming an essentially market-directed process. Both Marshall Crowe and James Schlesinger stressed that this trend will be fostered if future Canadian-U.S. energy relations are governed by pragmatism rather than grand energy strategies—national or continental.

Pragmatism may be a useful guide generally to the evolution of Canadian-U.S. relations. Unless restrictive policies are consciously adopted to reverse course, underlying forces are developing toward a continental marketplace for goods and services. Macroeconomic policy linkages are also strong. Canada is hardly in a position today to follow an independent monetary policy; and the United States, for all its size and economic power, will have to modify its fiscal and monetary stance to restore balance to its external accounts. This trend, Ambassador Gotlieb predicts, will generate new problems and disagreements having to do with such matters as how gains are shared and whether Canada's cultural identity and economic independence are threatened. In his view these costs of increasing economic integration are not reasons to halt the process but rather to seek innovative means—pragmatic means—to reconcile interests.

Initiatives for additional bilateral agreements on free trade within sectors, for bilateral reductions of nontariff barriers, and for bilateral agreements on the flow of services will advance this process. To some participants such limited initiatives seem too puny to be worth the effort; far better to strike out for a full-blown free-trade arrangement from the start. This position, it should be emphasized, is more a political than an economic judgment. If the officials of the two governments are right, politics favors the step-by-step approach. In the end the outcome could well be the same.

It is important, however, that expanded free trade up to and including a full bilateral free-trade area should not divert Canada and the United States from pushing for multilateral negotiation on goods and services later in the decade. Whatever is done bilaterally should be designed for ready extension multilaterally. Both countries could gain substantially from completing the multilateral process, and both would lose substantially if these bilateral arrangements served to weaken the multilateral system. This conclusion holds for the politics as well. For Canada the extension of global free trade would be the most effective means of allaying concerns about losing its national autonomy as a result of preclusive economic relations with the United States. For the United States, a strong multilateral trading system is an essential means of advancing its interests, which are inevitably global in character.

Premises of the Relationship

Canada's Independence and U.S. Domination

MITCHELL SHARP

In 1968, about the time I became secretary of state for external affairs in the government of Canada, George Ball wrote in *The Discipline of Power*:

> Canada, I have long believed, is fighting a rearguard action against the inevitable. Living next to our nation, with a population ten times as large as theirs and a gross national product fourteen times as great, the Canadians recognize their need for United States capital; but at the same time they are determined to maintain their economic and political independence. Their position is understandable, and the desire to maintain their national integrity is a worthy objective. But the Canadians pay heavily for it and, over the years, I do not believe they will succeed in reconciling the intrinsic contradiction of their position. I wonder, for example, if the Canadian people will be prepared indefinitely to accept, for the psychic satisfaction of maintaining a separate national and political identity, a per capita income less than three-fourths of ours. The struggle is bound to be a difficult one and I suspect, over the years, a losing one. Meanwhile there is danger that the efforts of successive Canadian governments to prevent United States economic domination will drive them toward increasingly restrictive nationalistic measures that are good neither for Canada nor for the health of the whole trading world.
>
> Thus, while I can understand the motivating assumptions of the Canadian position, I cannot predict a long life expectancy for her present policies. The great land mass to the south exerts an enormous gravitational attraction while at the same time tending to repel, and even without the divisive elements of a second culture in Quebec, the resultant strains and pressures are hard to endure. Sooner or later, commercial imperatives will bring about free movement of all goods back and forth across our long border; and when that occurs, or even before it does, it will become unmistakably clear that countries with economies so inextricably intertwined must also have free movement of the other vital factors of production, capital, services and labor. The result will inevitably be substantial economic integration, which will require for its full realization a progressively expanding area of common political decision.

At the time, these remarks were resented by a number of Canadians, and George Ball may have recanted. I recall them because whether one agrees or disagrees with his conclusions he was addressing the central issue in the Canadian-U.S. relationship.

George Ball is one of the few American statesmen who has said anything significant about that relationship in his memoirs. In *Years of Upheaval,* covering his tenure as secretary of state, Henry Kissinger made two glancing references to Canada. In *The White House Years* his comments on Canada were more substantial and understanding, but they were brief and largely descriptive. Zbigniew Brzezinski, although he had lived and taught in Canada for a time, said nothing about Canada in *Power and Principle.* In *Hard Choices,* Cyrus Vance mentioned Canada as one of five members of the UN Security Council trying to achieve Namibian independence, and that is all. President Carter paid tribute to Ken Taylor's part in rescuing six Americans in Tehran and mentioned Canadian participation in discussions about the energy crisis and the U.S. embargo on grain to the Soviet Union. I could not find any reference to Canada in the index to President Nixon's memoirs.

Is Canada "fighting a rearguard action against the inevitable"? I can understand how George Ball was led to this interpretation of events in Canada. It is very difficult for anyone, and particularly for outside observers however well informed and acute in their perceptions, to penetrate below the surface of the neverending debate in Canada about Canadian-U.S. relations, and it would be presumptuous to say that I can do this. What I shall present is an alternative interpretation of events that I believe comes closer to reality.

Intertwined economies

When I was growing up, Canada was still in some respects a British colony, although it was largely self-governing. The aim of Canadian nationalists in those days was to achieve full independence within the empire, or the Commonwealth as it later became. A dollar currency tied to the U.S. dollar rather than to the pound sterling was evidence of this independence. A shift toward the United States in trade and in the source of capital imports was evidence of Canada's growing maturity, its ability to stand on its own feet internationally. For Canada to be considered as an independent North American country with a British connection—indeed, as a bridge between London and Washington, as some contended—gave the nationalists of those days much satisfaction. Closer relations with the United States played an essential constructive role in the evolution of Canada from colony to nation.

No one now doubts Canada's independent status among nations except perhaps a few people who do not understand how Elizabeth can be at one and the same time queen of Great Britain and Canada, two independent countries. I am sure, however, that Americans like George Ball, steeped in the doctrine of separation of powers, admire our constitutional ingenuity.

It is also well to remember that in the post–World War II period, accessibility to U.S. capital, know-how, and markets helped turn Canada into one of the leading industrial nations of the world, with a standard of living surpassed only by that of our southern neighbor. As Europe and Japan recovered from the effects of the war, Canada's ranking changed; nevertheless, it has remained significant enough for the Canadian prime minister to merit a place at the summit of industrialized nations.

The Canadian and American economies have thus become closely intertwined. The countries are each other's leading trade partners, their mutual trade last year amounting to $149 billion. Americans have a big stake in the ownership of Canadian industry. And Canadian investments in the United States are also very large. So great is the interdependence between our two economies that economic trends in the United States find their reflection immediately in Canada. Finally, the U.S. presence in Canada's cultural life is massive.

Canadian reactions to U.S. dominance

This intertwining is at the heart of the debate that goes on in Canada about Canadian-U.S. relations. Canadians know that they have benefited and continue to benefit enormously from proximity to the United States. At the same time, they have become increasingly concerned—and I mean Canadians generally, not only the so-called Canadian nationalists—about the consequences of the dominant position of the United States in Canada's economy and in its cultural life for Canada's national independence, its sense of identity.

Over the years since the end of the war, I have watched that debate at close range as adviser to governments and have participated in it when I entered politics myself and became minister of the Crown with policy responsibilities. When I look back I am struck by the continuing ambiguity of the outcome. Canadians have never come down clearly on one side or the other. In the final analysis, we have usually managed to achieve a reasonable balance in our relationship with the United States. From time to time Canada has taken measures to stem the tide of Americanization, but they have never been such as to alter in any significant way the basic structure of the relationship between the two countries.

Nor, in my view, has it been the threat of U.S. retaliation that has tempered the enthusiasm of the economic nationalists. The opposition to extreme measures is internal; it comes from Canadians who are equally committed to the survival of Canada but who believe independence is compatible with close and mutually advantageous economic relations with the United States.

This is the reason I am skeptical about predictions that Canada is fighting a rearguard action against the inevitable. That is not what is going on. There is no reason to doubt that a very high proportion of Canadians want to remain Canadian. They are by no means convinced, however, that their best chance of survival as a separate country with its own institutions is to resort to measures that threaten seriously the advantages of proximity to the United States.

Viewed from the outside, Canadian–U.S. relations appear fuzzy and difficult to define, and so they are. So are federal-provincial relations within Canada, particularly relations between the French-speaking and the English-speaking societies. Canadians are a people who strive for compromise and tolerate a good deal of ambiguity. Only last year did we finally succeed in bringing our constitution home from Great Britain.

Canadian actions to regulate relations

If Canada is not fighting a rearguard action against the inevitability of absorption into the United States, what is going on? My assessment is that underlying our ambiguous attitude is a belief that if we play our cards carefully, we have the resources and the skills to enable us to take our place as an advanced industrial economy alongside the United States but less in the shadow of our great neighbor. Our national motivation is a positive one, not a negative one based simply on resistance to American domination.

I am inclined to agree with George Ball that if the Canadian approach were essentially a negative one, the main ingredients of which were increasingly restrictive barriers to investment and trade with the United States, it would probably lead to such strains that the approach would have to be abandoned. That is not, however, the way I perceive Canadian policy, and therefore I take a different view of the outcome.

Considering the dimensions of the domination of Canadian

industry by Americans and the degree of interdependence of our two economies, what is significant is not that Canada has taken some measures of a nationalistic kind but that those measures have, on the whole, been so moderate. For example, whatever one thinks of the existence of the Foreign Investment Review Agency (FIRA) and the resulting approval procedure, no one would claim that FIRA review has prevented Americans or other foreigners from investing in worthwhile projects in Canada, although it has probably altered the form and content of some of the investments and prevented some takeovers.

Even the National Energy Policy (NEP), which represented a departure from the accepted pattern, can now be seen for what it was: an effort on the part of the Canadian government to cope with the consequences of a very rapid increase in petroleum prices, consequences which, as it turned out, did not materialize. I recognize that there may be aspects of the program that justify criticism, but the NEP did not signal a fundamental change in Canadian policy toward foreign investment in general. It was a special case.

Canada's treatment of foreign banking institutions has also been moderate. In 1966 when I was minister of finance, I introduced legislation to require foreign banks to Canadianize themselves before being permitted to compete on an equal basis with Canadian-owned and -controlled banks. The target at that time was one foreign-owned bank. In due course these restrictions were somewhat liberalized, and now there are a substantial number of foreign banks, more than fifty-eight I am told, in Canada and competing with Canadian banks. Although they are still subject to some limitations, these limitations are now under review and may be relaxed. Such actions hardly represent rampant nationalism.

Canada has also taken steps to prevent its newspapers and television stations from being taken over by foreigners. The government has made it more expensive for Canadian companies to direct their advertising to a Canadian audience from U.S. TV stations on the border rather than from Canadian stations. Through tax measures it has given preference to Canadians who advertise in Canadian periodicals rather than in Canadian editions of U.S. magazines. But Canada has never placed any restrictions on the flow of American newspapers and magazines, and it is inundated by U.S. TV programs on its own networks as well as directly and through cable systems.

Consider also what has been going on in trade relations between

Canada and the United States. As a result of the successive rounds of negotiations under the aegis of the General Agreement on Tariffs and Trade (GATT), tariff barriers between Canada and the United States are only a small fraction of what they once were, and many commodities now move across the border free of any tariff. Equally significant is the willingness of the Canadian government to discuss the possibility of sectoral free-trade arrangements in specific commodities or groups of commodities, a willingness inspired by the example of the auto pact, which has been in existence for almost twenty years. A few years ago the emphasis was on trade diversification; today, although diversification is not forgotten, the efforts of Canadian government and business to promote trade are directed at the U.S. market, which is leading the recovery from the recession.

Free trade and Canadian independence

From time to time, proposals have been made for a North American free-trade area that would eliminate all barriers to cross-border trade, at least for industrial goods. The argument is made that because there are now so few barriers to trade, the elimination of the remaining barriers would not be a revolutionary step in the Canadian-U.S. relationship. These proposals have never been pushed to a conclusion, and the reason is that entering into such an exclusive trading relationship has more than economic implications. It would represent a political statement of integration with the U.S. economy. The question that has to be asked is whether such a move would be compatible with meaningful independence for Canada.

I discussed this point at some length in "Canada-U.S. Relations: Options for the Future," which I wrote in 1972. It has attained a certain notoriety and is popularly known in Canada as the Third Option paper.* I shall not repeat all the reasons why I did not favor the second option and, more particularly, why I had doubts about a free-trade area arrangement, but the essence of my position was as follows:

> A free-trade area arrangement . . . with the United States would, to all intents and purposes, be irreversible for Canada once embarked

* Ed. note: This article was published in a special issue of *International Perspectives*, Autumn 1972, by the Ministry of External Affairs, Canada. The three options were that
—Canada can seek to maintain more or less its present relationship with the United States with a minimum of policy adjustments;
—Canada can move deliberately toward closer integration with the United States;
—Canada can pursue a comprehensive long-term strategy to develop and strengthen the Canadian economy and other aspects of its national life, and in the process to reduce the present Canadian vulnerability.

upon. It would, theoretically, protect us against future changes in U.S. trade policy towards the rest of the world, though not against changes in U.S. domestic economic policy. This option has been rejected in the past because it was judged to be inconsistent with Canada's desire to preserve a maximum degree of independence, not because it lacked economic sense in terms of Canadian living standards and the stability of the Canadian economy. . . .

Internationally, there is a real risk that the conclusion of a free-trade arrangement between Canada and the United States would be taken as setting the seal upon the polarization of world trade. To the extent that it was, our room for bargaining with third countries would inevitably be reduced and our economic fortunes become more closely linked with those of the United States.

The experience of free-trade areas (such as the European Free Trade Association) suggests, in any case, that they tend to evolve toward more organic arrangements and the harmonization of internal economic policies. More specifically, they tend towards a full customs and economic union as a matter of internal logic. A Canadian-U.S. free-trade area would be almost certain to do likewise. Indeed, such a course could be argued to be in the Canadian interest because, to compete, we would probably require some harmonization of social and economic costs.

Several distinguished Canadians and prestigious organizations have taken the contrary view and have supported the idea of a free-trade area. What is significant to me is that no elected member of Parliament has done so. As a former politician, I understand why. To enter into a free-trade area arrangement with the United States is to alter fundamentally the direction of Canadian policy, not so much in economic terms as in political terms, and Canadians are not prepared to do so.

If Canadians were a poor people, making little progress, living next to rich Americans, and resenting the disparity, the future of Canada as an independent nation might be more doubtful and the pressures toward absorption harder to resist. But the fact is that by international standards Canada is well off, and in the postwar period its national income has increased at about the same rate as that of the United States, although the average per capita figure remains significantly lower. Even if Canada entered into a free-trade arrangement, the gap might not be significantly reduced. In any event, national income is high enough to enable Canadians to finance, without too much difficulty, programs of public expenditure for education, social services, and the arts that compare favorably with similar programs in the United States. Consequently, Canada does not suffer in any real sense of the word from maintaining its independence. Canadians look forward to improving their conditions of life, just as Americans look forward to improving theirs and, of course, subject to the same uncertainties.

Sometimes it must be difficult for Americans doing business in Canada to understand Canadian peculiarities or even to accept the fact that we are different and want to remain different. Canada seems very similar to the United States—American magazines in the shops, American television programs, McDonald's hamburgers. Like the rest of the world and, because of proximity, to a greater degree than any other country, Canada has been powerfully affected by U.S. enterprise and popular culture. But appearances can be deceiving. Under the surface, Canada is a country with a different history: no Revolution or Civil War, parliamentary rather than an executive-congressional government, a different kind of federalism resulting from the existence of a French-speaking, fiercely proud society, a greater willingness to accept authority, and a more positive attitude toward the responsibilities of government. Patriotic fervor is not the Canadian style. We have no heroes like Washington or Lincoln. It took us a hundred years to decide to have our own flag. We have learned over the years to recognize not only the necessity but the value in a healthy democracy of diversity—in language, in culture, in regional characteristics. That is what preserves Canadian unity and contributes to our pride of country and sense of national achievement. It is a quiet pride.

So, in the years ahead, I foresee continued close economic relations between Canada and the United States. This makes sense for both countries and is not, in my view, incompatible with Canadian independence. Indeed, as the interdependence of all economies continues to grow, the Canadian-U.S. relationship will appear less exceptional. I do not think it likely, however, that Canada will choose deliberate economic integration with the United States in the form of a free-trade area, although there may well be a further reduction in the already low barriers to trade. Canada will continue to take measures to control foreign investment, to encourage Canadian ownership, and to offset the powerful American influences on our cultural life, but Canadians are too sensible to support policies that would interfere in any significant way with economic development.

I can also predict with confidence that the Canadian-U.S. relationship will not always be full of sweetness and light. There will be times when Canada differs with U.S. policies. We never broke relations with Cuba, for instance, and we were years ahead of the United States in recognizing the People's Republic of China. Today Canadians have misgivings about some aspects of U.S. foreign and defense policies. There will be times when we feel, as we do now, that some of our interests are overlooked: acid rain is a case in point. There will be times when Canada's efforts to resist being overwhelmed by American power and influence will cause concern in the United States. But Canadian policies will never be inspired by anti-Americanism.

Relations at the official level

One final issue is Canadian-U.S. relations at the official level. For Canada the relationship with the United States is at the very center of economic, environmental, defense, and political concerns. For the United States the relationship is not similarly important, notwithstanding what successive presidents have said about giving priority to good relations with America's closest neighbors. As a great power and leader of the West, the United States has bigger problems to worry about in this turbulent world.

I do not yearn for a return to that special relationship when we had a joint cabinet committee of senior Canadian ministers and U.S. secretaries that met periodically to review the relationship. Those simpler days are gone forever. Nor do I underestimate the efforts that have been made in the U.S. State Department to give Canadian affairs a higher profile among their general concerns. It gives Canadians reassurance to know that the present U.S. secretary of state meets four times a year with the present Canadian secretary of state for external affairs.

But what seems to me to be lacking—and let me be clear that I am speaking about the official level of contacts, not the private level—is a systematic approach to Canadian-U.S. relations. Considering the enormous volume of transactions across the border and the complex web of interrelationships that exist, the approach of the governments to each other is surprisingly ad hoc and problem-oriented.

This may be inevitable. I have been secretary of state for external affairs; I know how difficult it is to bring together all the strands of the relationship and review them as a whole. The temptation is to say that if there are no pressing problems in a particular field, why bother? Let's concentrate on the pressure points. The increase in contacts between the two countries at the legislative level, between Canadian parliamentarians and U.S. senators and congressmen and between the Canadian ambassador and members of the U.S. Congress, has very naturally concentrated on such grievances and points of conflict as are uppermost at the time.

Doesn't the unique nature of the relationship, however, call for establishing a unique form of periodic and regular consultation, particularly on economic matters, that includes but goes beyond traditional diplomatic channels? What I have in mind is not the creation of new machinery for consultation on Canadian-U.S. relations; like many others I am skeptical about new committees for any purpose. The need, it seems to me, is to make more systematic use of the existing machinery and the official channels of communication.

Specifically, I suggest that periodically, and at least once a year, each government should review from its own point of view relations with the other—economic, political, defense, the whole spectrum of relations—put its observations and conclusions on a piece of paper, and hand the paper to the other for review in advance of a meeting attended by the appropriate secretaries, ministers and officials. The purpose would be to ensure that the issues in the relationship are not overlooked by the U.S. government, concerned as it is with its global responsibilities; to put these issues into perspective so that they are neither exaggerated nor minimized; and to minimize the possibility of misunderstanding. In preparing its paper, the Canadian government could use the occasion to consult with private interests, as could the U.S. government in preparing its paper.

Other and better methods for more systematic consultation may be available. In view of the complexity of the Canadian-U.S. interrelationship, however, I am convinced that we need something special in addition to the ad hoc approach now being followed.

Overview of Canadian-U.S. Relations

GEORGE W. BALL

I AM ALWAYS gratified to find that anyone has read one of my books, but I can assure Mitchell Sharp that there is no great danger of cultural domination by the United States. While I wrote that book in 1968, nobody mentioned it or noticed it in Canada until three years later. At that time, some obscure editorial writer happened to chance on it, noticed those observations, and wrote an editorial about them. Within about three days I had suddenly become notorious in Canada, and many people were saying some rude things about me. This was not what I had intended. In any event, it was a passing storm.

When I wrote those comments I was still preoccupied with what had occurred in Europe, the movement toward forming the European Economic Community. Some of us who had worked on the origins of the community believed that a free-trade area, as embodied in a common market and its institutions, would indeed be a political statement. We definitely had political objectives in mind. In time, we fervently hoped, the European Community would lead to the erosion of national sovereignty as it had existed in Europe for so many centuries.

That has not happened, much to my disappointment. The high expectations we had of a strong movement toward political unity have not been borne out. At that time, however, I believed that the evolution I foresaw occurring in Europe might repeat itself in North America. Moving toward a free-trade area (not a common market because I thought a common external tariff was unlikely) would have exactly the effect that Mitchell Sharp mentioned; it would constitute a political statement and be followed by progress toward political unity. But in view of the experience of Europe, I fear that kind of political statement is not very effective. I find a resurgence, not an erosion, of nationalism in Europe today.

American complaints about Canada

I shall try to avoid repeating the clichés that are used to describe relations between the United States and Canada. I shall not even mention what every schoolchild knows—or did know when our

21

schools still taught geography—that our two countries share the longest undefended border in the world. What we are concerned with at this meeting is that, though we do not shoot across that border, we often shout across it. There are complaints, often querulous complaints, emanating from both sides. I hope we can sort some of them out in our discussions.

Americans have long grumbled about Canada's efforts to husband its resources and move toward a greater degree of autarchy. Canadians, we frequently complain, do not always recognize their full share of responsibility for our common defense. Finally—and such conduct seems most inexcusable—Canada often insists on pursuing foreign policies that differ from those solemnly pronounced by Washington.

During the years when I was in the Department of State, for example, the Canadians had the audacity to recognize and trade with China even after we had made clear that America regarded China as an "evil empire" and "focus of evil"—or whatever theological epithets we used at that time. Because we Americans knew wrong from right, we imposed a tight embargo that precluded any supping with the devil. But the Canadians were unrepentant. Indeed, the Canadian government even got upset when we tried to save it from a grievous sin by seeking to block the Canadian Wheat Board from fulfilling Chinese orders for Canadian wheat. At the goading of a zealous lady who had been in charge of such matters ever since the days of William McKinley, the U.S. Treasury directed an American company to refuse to let its Canadian subsidiary make available some portable wheat-loading equipment that could not be obtained elsewhere. Of course, our government finally relented under pressure, but that did not excuse the wicked behavior of the Canadians in prematurely pursuing a foreign policy position it took us another decade to adopt.

Canadian reactions to the United States

But if we Americans frequently grumble about Canada, the Canadians are even more vehement in criticizing Americans for paying too little attention to Canadian views and policies. What most disturbs Canadians is that Americans tend to take Canada for granted, that they make little effort to learn about Canadian problems and activities that do not directly touch their lives. They point out, with good reason, that the American press largely ignores events in Canada compared with far less significant occurrences in other nations. As reassurance I would only point out that that is primarily because Canada is not constantly engaged in bombing and shooting at people, for there is certainly no consistent correlation between American press coverage and the size or importance of nations. Israel, for example, with its 4 million inhabitants, receives substantially more coverage in the major eastern newspapers than do the nations of Europe or even the Soviet Union. Nevertheless, I think the Canadians do have a legitimate grievance at what amounts to deplorable American parochialism.

Another complaint is that Americans own too large a share of the Canadian economy, and various Canadian governments have sought to redress the balance—particularly with respect to natural resources. Still another set of complaints involves such esoteric matters as fishing rights and such environmental problems as acid rain.

I think Americans would be more sensitive to Canada's special concerns if they thought Canadians noticeably different from their own countrymen. Except in Quebec, Canadians and Americans speak the same language, although Canadians do not always know how to pronounce the word "house." But because Canadians look and talk like we do and because we share much the same cultural background and the same values and live in very much the same way, we tend to take it for granted that our two peoples necessarily think within a common frame of reference. Thus those of us who live in the United States all too often show a lamentable insensitivity to the fierce concern of Canadians to maintain a distinct identity, which sometimes manifests itself in a strong reaction to thoughtless American encroachments on Canada's sovereignty.

Americans tend to think, for example, that it would be only logical to develop a common plan for the exploitation of North America's natural resources, particularly since Canada has such a rich stock of them. Canadians, on the other hand, benightedly believe that they have the right to husband their resources and use them in a manner that best serves their national interests. Unfortunately we Americans are made aware of that divergence of view only when there are crises. Most of the time we think of Canadians as substantially less nationalistic than Texans.

We compound the confusion by failing to recognize that Canadians live under institutions that differ substantially from ours. Canada is not, after all, a federation but a confederation, and provincial governments have far more autonomy than the governments of American states. Thus we fail to appreciate that the government in Ottawa must strive constantly to achieve compromises and strengthen national ties. Yet, although most Americans may be unaware of this structural distinction, some are prepared to take advantage of it. Our intrepid oil producers often act as though the premier of Alberta were more powerful than the premier of Canada.

The evolution of relations

The evolution of Canadian-U.S. relations since World War II has been marked by major changes and occasional crises. At the end of the war Canada still maintained strong and special ties to Great Britain as a member of the Commonwealth. Those ties have gradually diminished under the pressure of new economic and political realities, but still, as late as the early 1960s during my years in the State Department, Commonwealth preferences created some problems between us. The United States was trying to encourage Britain to bite the bullet and join the European Economic Community, while Canada was concerned at the effect on its light industries if Britain were to subject itself to the common external tariff of the community.

Our relations were also troubled by the understandable desire to maintain its cultural integrity that led Canada to adopt measures that discouraged the circulation of American periodicals and generated a prickly dispute. Under the conditions that prevail today, however, no open society can insulate itself from the flow of ideas across national borders. In western Canada particularly, one feels the powerful thrust of American newspapers and television; the flow of traffic and ideas seems to move more intensively north-south than east-west. Canada is only now building strong east-west ties that have been complicated by weather, topography, the vast distances involved, and the uneven distribution of population.

For a quarter century after the war a succession of U.S. governments tried to mitigate their problems with Canada by according Canada special exemptions and immunities, and—at least when they thought of it—they consulted with Ottawa before taking actions or adopting policies that might adversely affect Canadian interests. For example, the United States made an exception for Canada under the Marshall Plan when it permitted recipients to spend their aid funds in Canada as well as the United States. Another instance occurred in 1963 when the Kennedy administration, of which I was then a part, faced a succession of balance of payments deficits (though, by today's standards, those deficits were miniscule). Half of the deficit in 1963 was accounted for by foreign borrowing in the New York money market, and Canadian firms, municipalities, and provincial governments had been the issuers of 67 percent of all new foreign securities taken up during the first six months of the year. To reduce foreign borrowings, the U.S. Treasury proposed in July 1963 to impose an interest equalization tax that would raise the effective interest cost to foreigners by about 1.25 percent.

Strange as it may seem, none of us on the American side had anticipated the intensity of the Canadian reaction to that proposed tax. Between noon and one o'clock on the day of the announcement a selling wave on the Toronto Stock Exchange was triggered by the fear that American investors would sell off their Canadian portfolios, and the following morning saw the sharpest declines ever recorded in the history of the Toronto Stock Exchange. Faced with these declines, a most impressive Canadian delegation descended on Washington, and on Saturday afternoon we met with Walter Gordon, Mitchell Sharp's predecessor as finance minister, and a substantial number of others. The Canadian arguments were cogent and impressive and I think all of us felt some chagrin that we had not fully appreciated how closely the capital markets of our two countries were integrated.

As a result we worked out a compromise that permitted $350 million a year of Canadian security issues to be sold free of tax, with the understanding that Canada would limit the buildup of its foreign exchange reserves to a certain figure. Moreover, the president retained the discretion to fix the limit below $350 million at any time. All that caused considerable soul searching on the Canadian side, for it meant that Canada's freedom to use monetary policy to control inflation would be constrained. In effect, that policy would be tied to the decisions of the Federal Reserve Board, because if Canada moved interest rates too high in order to restrain inflationary pressures, American funds would flow into Canada and thus raise Canadian exchange reserves beyond the permissible level.

Those in the government who participated in the talks with Canada at that time learned a solemn lesson. The next time, during the Johnson administration, that we imposed new curbs on investment abroad, we cleared the draft regulations with Canada and made the changes needed to satisfy the Canadian government.

If America was responding to its domestic concerns by limiting the outflow of funds, the Canadian government was also contemplating restrictive policies. Under the leadership of its finance minister, Walter Gordon, Canada began in 1963 to reexamine its whole relationship with the United States. Gordon recommended a 30 percent tax on the value of Canadian firms that were taken over by U.S. subsidiaries and a tax on dividends that depended on the degree to which a firm was owned by foreigners. Even though Parliament did not enact these measures, they seemed to us in Washington to reflect a major departure from previous policy. And those anxieties were to continue. Thereafter we watched the creation of the Foreign Investment Review Agency (FIRA), the efforts of Saskatchewan to expropriate the potash industry and of Quebec to take over the asbestos industry, and finally the announcement of the National Energy Program. All this made clear that from the Canadian point of view there was nothing very special about relations with the United States and that Canada was becoming as restrictive of foreign investments as many other countries.

On the American side the symbolic breakdown of the special relationship occurred in 1971 when President Nixon refused to exempt Canada from the 10 percent import surtax. Because that was a sharp break with the way we treated Canada at the time of the interest equalization tax, the meaning would have been clear even without formal amplification; but President Nixon and Secretary of State Kissinger made it explicit that the days were over when Canada could expect any exemption from America's financial and economic measures. Even so, under President Carter, we did except Canada as well as Mexico from the effects of the convention tax.

Future relations

I do not intend to recount history or to describe all of the problems that Canada and the United States have faced as a result of the interaction of their economic policies. The views of the Canadian democracy have evolved erratically, but so have the views of the U.S. democracy. That, I think, is a characteristic of popularly elected governments. From time to time we have heard brave comments from Canada about its Third Option, which Mitchell Sharp put forth. There have been increasing grumblings on the American side with what are viewed as protectionist overtones in Canadian policies. Yet we have together achieved some very significant breakthroughs such as, for example, the Automotive Parts Agreement, which was, as many of us recognized, a magnificent tour de force brought about by Philip Trezise, as far as the American side was concerned. And we now hear promising talk of new sectoral free-trade arrangements.

I like to think, since I have myself survived for a very long while, that wisdom comes from age and experience and that the longer our two great nations exist side by side, the more sensitive we shall each become with regard to the other's problems. That is, I suggest, more than a pious wish; it is essential if we are both to prosper.

We have a good chance of achieving that. Mitchell Sharp has proposed an interesting mechanism for systematic consultation. I once proposed that we should try to develop ground rules for U.S. relations with Canada—accepted principles to guide us. This resulted in the Merchant-Heeney Report, which was an attempt to put some ground rules on paper. As with so many other ventures of that kind, the result turned out to be too abstract to be of great practical value. Nevertheless consultation is not merely a useful idea but a practical necessity.

I am sorry to hear that we have abandoned the practice of annual cabinet meetings. I thought they were very useful. We used to work hard at them. While comments at times were sharp, we derived a lot of benefit from them. And consultation, to be useful, has to be systematized. Meeting only in times of crisis is not good enough.

Mitchell Sharp suggested I might have recanted from the heretical views I put forward in 1968. In my defense I will say only that they were misinterpreted in Canada. I was simply, in a rather daydreaming way, making a prediction. Based on what has happened in Europe, I now think that it is a less and less likely prediction, namely, that the underlying logic of our common positions would require our two countries to move toward a greater degree of unity.

I learned in the reaction to that idea about the fierce sense of national identity that the Canadian people feel, and I commend them for it. I was misunderstood, however, in the Canadian assumption that I was advocating a course of action that would lead to a kind of union of our two countries. When I had to defend myself in Canada, I tried to explain that I was not advocating such a course of action. In fact, I thought that very few Americans would want this to happen, once they examined all the implications, principally because it would upset the political balance in a way that would mean the rewriting of American politics.

General Discussion

ROBERT MATHIESON of AT&T asked whether new sectoral agreements between Canada and the United States would be neutral with respect to multilateral agreements on trade and investment.

Sharp said he hoped so and that we should not abandon the multilateral approach. He understood that every effort would be made in the sectoral negotiations to avoid compromising that position.

Robert Dunn, Jr., of George Washington University questioned the idea that a free-trade area would be threatening to Canada politically because it would be analogous to the European Community (EC). He thought the analogy was not with the EC, which had political objectives, but with the European Free Trade Association (EFTA), which did not. He also speculated that interest in a Canadian-U.S. free-trade area stemmed partly from the fact that the economic adjustments would be comparatively easy to make. Canada and the United States have similar wage scales and price relationships. As a result, no major interest groups in either country would be seriously threatened by a free-trade arrangement. In contrast a free-trade arrangement with Mexico, where differences in factor costs are very large, would require much more difficult economic adjustments.

Sharp said that the political problem with a free-trade area between Canada and the United States rests on the relative size of the partners. That differentiates it from the European situation. It would be a political statement of a kind that Canada has never made. Once made, it would be irreversible. It would say that Canada does not believe it could make its way in a multilateral world and therefore must join one of the big players.

Instead of two countries of relatively equal size deciding to join in a free-trade area, Canada, already dominated by the American economy and by American culture, would seem to be getting into bed with the United States permanently. That would be the

28

nature of the decision, and that differentiated it from similar arrangements in Europe.

Bruce MacLaury pointed out that some of the partners within EFTA or in the EC are relatively small but nevertheless apparently believe they have something to gain and specifically do not seem to believe they will suffer a loss of political identity in the process. He therefore argued that Sharp's comment about comparative size as the crucial distinction was relevant but not totally convincing.

Sharp responded that the economic combinations in Europe involved more than two countries.

Ball commented that in theory a free-trade area would have some restrictive effect on national economic policies. In practice, most countries had the ingenuity to find ways and means to get around those constraints and maintain a very considerable amount of autonomy in national economic policies. This was true even within the EC.

In general, there could be some virtue in not trying to move toward a free-trade area overnight, particularly because of Canadian political concerns. A sectoral approach might be a better way to start because sooner or later the logic would call for a broader approach.

This was a lesson Ball said that he learned in Europe. In working with Jean Monnet on the creation of the Coal and Steel Community, he recognized that subjecting one particular economic sector to a special regime was illogical. Nonetheless, he believed that logic would eventually compel the Europeans to expand the concept to the entire economic sector, which indeed is what happened.

David Leyton-Brown of York University commented that in formulating his Third Option, Sharp primarily wanted to reduce Canadian economic vulnerability to the United States. Yet in his remarks at the conference, Sharp acknowledged that although trade diversification was by no means a forgotten concern, present Canadian trade promotion efforts were directed at the American market because the United States was leading the recovery from the recession. He asked, therefore, whether Sharp now believed that Canadian vulnerability to the United States had been sufficiently reduced, or whether the short-term priority of recovering from the recession overwhelmed any longer-term consideration of vulnerability, or if there were some third position that neither of the first two would sufficiently cover.

Sharp said that the purpose or at least the theme of the paper on the Third Option was not trade diversification and that very little was said about it there. Trade diversification was consistent, however, with the Third Option. He did not believe the vulnerability of the Canadian economy had been reduced. If anything, Canada was even more vulnerable than it was in 1972 when the paper was written. He argued that Canadians would inevitably try to follow the Third Option, successfully or not. Rather than seek integration with the United States or follow an ad hoc approach, Canadian policy should seek to reduce vulnerability to events outside Canada, particularly those in the United States. Little has been done to follow such an approach because it is extremely difficult in Canada to carry out an industrial strategy. The provinces rather than the federal government largely control the operation.

Although little had happened, Sharp continued to see merit in a systematic policy directed to maintaining the independence of Canada.

MacLaury pointed out that all industrial countries are more vulnerable to external developments than they were ten years ago. To counter this secular trend would require strenuous actions and policies going against the strong underlying economic forces that are shrinking the economic world. Is it therefore, he wondered, a matter of national policy, followed or not, or a matter of secular trends in markets that are working in the opposite direction, that is, in increasing economic vulnerability generally?

Sharp acknowledged this point. His position might have been stated too restrictively. To some extent the Canadian government has tried to follow the Third Option, but perhaps it has been overwhelmed by the tendencies toward greater interdependence among all countries in the world. That, he said, may be a more accurate statement.

Pierre-Paul Proulx of the Canadian Department of Regional Industrial Expansion asked Ball whether the unspoken premise of the sectoral free-trade negotiations was the concern in both Canada and the United States about the need to reverse the decline in their share of world trade. The competitive position of both countries had weakened. One possible response would be to address adjustment issues jointly. This would require an emphasis on the stronger economic sectors in both countries as candidates for bilateral free trade. Furthermore, he suggested, in the absence of a common external tariff, a full free-trade arrangement would be unstable, particularly because of pressures from trade with developing countries.

Ball responded that a free-trade area with no common external tariff could result in considerable administrative problems, particularly because of the large size of the two economies. As to the thesis that Canada and the United States are likely to experience a declining share of world commerce, Ball had some reservations. Whether the trend of the recent past would be interrupted was still an open question, particularly because many underlying factors were changing. In the United States productivity was now increasing, notably in some industries likely to be considered in the sectoral discussions. Ball doubted that decisions to move toward sectoral arrangements between the United States and Canada should be based very much on the assumption that these improvements in productivity will continue.

Allan Gotlieb, Canadian ambassador to the United States, asked Sharp whether in some ways Canadian vulnerability had been reduced in the past decade. Accepting the point that all countries are now more vulnerable because world economic interdependence has grown, he asked whether in a number of areas considered sensitive ten years ago, the sense of Canadian identity, unity, and sovereignty had not in fact strengthened. As an example, he cited the cultural area generally and the decline in the degree of foreign ownership in Canada. He wondered whether Sharp had not been too pessimistic in his assessment of these elements of change in Canada. He believed that Canadians now are more confident about their identity and their future prospects. This confidence may have affected their attitude toward free trade or sectoral free trade as well as their general attitude toward the United States and the world as a whole. Hasn't Canada emerged from the developments in the past decade with a greater degree of self-confidence?

Sharp agreed that in the past ten years Canada had developed a much greater sense of its identity in the theater, music, and the other arts. He questioned how this related to the economic issue.

In cultural affairs, Canada is finally reaping the benefits of past efforts. And progress has been made on the problem of excessive foreign ownership of Canadian industry. On the other hand, Canada is now more vulnerable to changes in American interest rates or to the size of the American deficit or to economic conditions generally in the United States. In these respects, Sharp argued, Canada shares in the growing interdependence of all economies.

Because Canadians feel more Canadian than ever before, they will resist any political move toward greater integration with the United States. Such a move is quite separate from becoming more interdependent, which would be determined by other events. But there would, if anything, be greater resistance to the idea of moving into the American sphere than there ever was in the past.

The last time an effort was made to promote a free-trade area was in 1948. Only the last-minute intervention of Prime Minister King (according to his diary) then prevented it from taking place. Nothing like that would happen again. Nothing would be done under the table or in secret.

MacLaury understood Gotlieb's comments in a different sense, namely that having achieved greater self-confidence, Canada had more leeway to move toward greater economic integration without feeling at risk culturally or politically.

Gotlieb said his remarks were not intended to lead in any direction. He had simply been trying to emphasize that considerable progress had been made in achieving a key part of Sharp's Third Option. In the broadest sense, Canadian vulnerability had been reduced—to the extent this was possible in the modern world. How Canadians would react to this change in shaping their external relations was still to be determined.

Trade and Investment Issues

The Issue of Free Trade

SIMON S. REISMAN

IN THIS EXPOSITION I propose to (1) review the major events in the history of Canadian-U.S. trade relations; (2) draw some lessons from these events that may help to illuminate current issues; (3) offer a view of the main economic consequences of free trade between our two countries; (4) outline the main economic obstacles and objections to free trade; and (5) suggest how a free-trade agreement may be structured so as to remove or at least reduce some of the more fundamental economic and political objections to such a regime.

I will not be dealing with investment issues as such, except where policies to control investment have their origin in trade relations. Nor will I be addressing current trade problems in any detail except, again, where they bear upon the broader question of free trade.

History of Canadian-U.S. trade

In Canada's commercial relations with the United States from pre-Confederation days to the present, no concept has carried as much weight or caused as much excitement—economic and political—as the term "reciprocity." I must be careful to distinguish immediately the historic meaning of reciprocity from the use to which this word is now being put in the U.S. Congress. As I understand it, reciprocity in recent congressional usage suggests trade restrictions and retaliation for unfair treatment of U.S. exports. By contrast, reciprocity in Canadian usage for almost 200 years has meant a policy directed to the mutual reduction of tariffs and other barriers to trade between Canada and the United States, although not necessarily on the same goods nor to the same degree. Historically, this concept has embraced everything from small tariff reductions affecting a few products to overall free trade. In a real sense the current discussions about sectoral free trade between Canada and the United States are in the tradition of reciprocity, as would be the case if the discussions were to broaden to embrace the creation of a free-trade area.

A good place to begin is the Elgin-Marcy Reciprocity Treaty

35

of 1854. It was born out of termination by Great Britain in 1846 of the old preferential arrangements between the mother country and her colonies that the original Province of Canada had enjoyed. Great Britain embarked on a policy of unilateral free trade at that time. Withdrawal of protection in the markets of the mother country had a severe impact on the province. In the ensuing years the Canadian colonies tried to reach a reciprocity agreement with the United States. Negotiations were protracted, and it was difficult to arouse much interest in the United States. But persistence and patience were finally rewarded after eight years of effort and after threats of raising barriers against U.S. goods. In the end it was a dispute over the boundary fisheries and not U.S. interests in promoting trade that brought matters to a head. Space does not permit a more complete review of the negotiations that led to the 1854 treaty, but it doubtless would be instructive to later Canadian negotiators to learn the need and the techniques for obtaining support from U.S. congressmen and senators by appealing to the special interests they represent.

The Reciprocity Treaty provided for free interchange between the United States and the British North American colonies of many natural products, including timber, grain, fish, animals, meat, butter, cheese, flour, and coal. Two-way trade flourished under these arrangements, but there were numerous complaints on both sides of the border about breaches of the agreement. Bitterness in the United States about certain Canadian tariff increases on manufactured goods—which, incidentally, were not covered by the treaty—and ill feeling against Canada generated during the Civil War led to unilateral abrogation of the treaty by the United States in 1866.

This was the only trade treaty in our commercial history that provided for free trade in broad sectors. Yet there has not been a time during the 118 years that have since elapsed when significant support on both sides of the border, but especially in Canada, could not be mustered for another reciprocity treaty. In 1869, 1871, and again in 1874 Canada made attempts, supported by almost all political leaders, to negotiate an agreement similar to Elgin-Marcy. There was little interest in the United States.

The 1874 effort is worthy of note. A draft treaty was negotiated with the United States that provided for the reciprocal free entry of natural products as under the 1854 treaty. But it also included reciprocal free entry of agricultural implements, steel, paper, locomotives, furniture, boots and shoes, wood manufactures, and a substantial number of other manufactured goods. The treaty was approved by the British government on behalf of the Dominion of Canada and only required the assent of the U.S. Senate to become effective. In the end it failed to obtain Senate approval. As J. H. Young's book, *Canadian Commercial Policy*, notes,

> Although it was not a matter of great importance to the United States to obtain an agreement with Canada, in a sense an opportunity was missed by the United States in 1874 which has not presented itself again. On a number of occasions attempts have been made to reach some kind of arrangement with the United States, but no Canadian government since 1874 has been prepared to include free entry on as wide a range of manufactured goods as that included in George Brown's draft treaty.

An interesting facet of the failed 1874 effort at reciprocity is that it was inspired by severely depressed economic conditions in Canada that had continued for some years. In 1879 a new government led by John A. Macdonald brought in the historic National Policy on a strong wave of nationalism and protectionism. In part at least, this was a response to rejection by the United States of efforts to achieve free trade. It was a drastic change in the commercial policy under which the British North American colonies had developed, and it became a major force affecting the economic development and industrial structure of the country that confederation had created.

The main lines of the protective system then introduced have never since been basically altered. But even the 1879 National Policy with its highly protective tariff did not signal a clear break with the attractive U.S. market to the south. The statute establishing the policy contained a provision for reciprocity with the United States in natural products. Thus the door was left open, and reciprocity, at least in this limited sense, was made part of the trade policy philosophy of both major political parties.

Two particular events in Canadian political history of that period had a significant bearing on reciprocity. The national election of 1891 was largely fought over a plank in the Liberal platform calling for "unrestricted reciprocity." Canadian nationalism, political independence, and the connection with the empire were worked to the limit by the incumbent prime minister, John A. Macdonald. He retained his majority handily. But reciprocity was not tested in negotiations for the next two decades and became a quiescent issue.

In 1911 the Laurier government again fought an election on reciprocity. The initiative had come from the United States and an agreement had been negotiated, not as a treaty but as something to be implemented by concurrent legislation. It had much of the content of the original 1854 Reciprocity Treaty but included some manufactured goods. There was also provision for equality of tariffs at a reduced rate on automobiles and agricultural implements. Reciprocity became the chief issue of the 1911 election, and the defeat of the Laurier government was interpreted as a defeat for the principle.

Despite two major electoral defeats on the reciprocity issue, the call of the U.S. market remained strong, and efforts were made at ministerial level to interest the United States in trade negotiations in 1922 and 1923. The United States at that time was moving in the direction of greater protection under the Fordney-McCumber tariff of 1922. To cap the trend, the Hawley-Smoot bill in 1930 raised the average tariff on dutiable imports to a prohibitive 53 percent in response to the onset of the Great Depression.

There the matter rested—with trade relations at their lowest ebb—until the Hull Trade Agreement Act of 1934 made possible two substantial agreements with Canada in 1935 and 1938. These were the first successful agreements since the abrogation of the 1854 Reciprocity Agreement. While they were not reciprocity agreements in the earlier sense, they did redress some of the carnage of Hawley-Smoot.

Little need be said about commercial relations between Canada and the United States during World War II. A high level of cooperation then existed between two friendly countries with common defense objectives. Sharing scarce raw materials, joint production programs for essential war goods, rationing, and allocation displaced the traditional peacetime trade instruments. An interesting trade advance did occur in 1944 when duties were removed in both countries on all agricultural machinery and implements. This category of goods has remained on the free list ever since.

What can be said about reciprocity in the post–World War II years? Many of us participated in the 1946–47 Geneva and Havana conferences for the establishment of an international trade organization. These efforts were stillborn, but the scrawny sibling of the proposed organization—the General Agreement on Tariffs and Trade—survived. Within the framework of the multilateral trade and tariff negotiations sponsored by GATT, Canada and the United States entered into a series of substantive agreements at Geneva, Annecy, and Torquay and also during the Dillon,

Kennedy, and Tokyo rounds of trade negotiations. But the very nature of the principal-supplier rule* governing the early negotiations and the proportionate cuts of the later efforts meant that with few exceptions there was little opportunity for negotiations between Canada and the United States for reciprocal free trade. The rates have been reduced substantially, however, in both countries' schedules. Indeed, with a few exceptions it is no longer the tariff that troubles Canada in its trade with the United States. Rather it is a range of U.S. nontariff barriers, emergency measures, and threats of restrictive action that creates the most severe problems for Canadian exports. Such barriers are less important for U.S. exports to Canada, where tariffs remain significant obstacles.

Two events in the postwar Canadian-U.S. trade relationship deserve special mention: the secret negotiations between officials of the two countries in Washington in 1947–48 to establish a free-trade area and the Canadian-U.S. Automotive Products Trade Agreement of 1965.

Little information on the 1947–48 secret talks for a free-trade area is available on the official public record from Canadian sources and, as far as I know, virtually nothing from U.S. sources. In Canada a semiofficial record is available in the form of cryptic diary entries reproduced in the Mackenzie King memoirs, volume four. There is also a brief unpublished account by a senior Canadian official who took part in the Washington talks. Various newspaper and journal articles appeared in both countries at the time, but their accuracy has never been officially confirmed. Finally, there is a journal article by a Canadian historian who drew on these sources as well as on interviews and departmental files, but it is incomplete and apparently not entirely accurate.

As best I can piece it together the story of the 1947–48 free-trade episode is as follows. The initiative to explore the possibility of a comprehensive free-trade arrangement came from the United

---

* Ed. note: The principal-supplier rule was a guide to the selection of products for negotiating tariff or other trade barrier reductions. Under the rule, the United States would negotiate on, say, steel products with the nation supplying the largest share of American imports of those products. Agreements reached in these paired, product-specific negotiations would then be extended to all GATT members in accord with the most-favored-nation clause. U.S. negotiations with Canada, therefore, were limited at maximum to those products of which one was principal supplier to the other. (The United States, moreover, was always subject to a legislated limit on the size of the tariff reductions its negotiators could offer.) In the Kennedy and Tokyo rounds the agreed objective was to achieve equal, across-the-board reductions on all products except those specifically identified as being exempted. This guideline in effect set a ceiling on the achievable cuts in tariffs.

States and was relayed to the prime minister through the minister of finance. The prime minister authorized the two most senior Canadian trade officials, Hector McKinnon and John Deutsch, to meet with their opposite numbers in Washington to explore the possibility of entering into a comprehensive free-trade agreement. The U.S. team included Clair Wilcox, Woodward Willoughby, Constant Southard, and other officials. Talks lasted several months, and the framework of an agreement, including detailed schedules, was drawn up. As time went by, however, it became clear that U.S. approval would be protracted, complex, and uncertain. The prime minister's early enthusiasm and strong support gave way to doubts that were reinforced by his advancing age, impending retirement, worry about burdening his successor with so large a task at the outset of his tenure, and by the impending U.S. election. In the end Mackenzie King decided not to proceed. The U.S. officials were informed of his decision in early May, and the talks were broken off. There the matter ended.

The circumstances of the 1947–48 free-trade talks may be instructive in considering the practicability, timing, and conditions of new free-trade initiatives. At that time Canada was in the midst of an exchange crisis that looked serious and likely to endure. The crisis arose out of a breakdown in traditional trade links with the United Kingdom and continental Europe. These countries could not afford to pay for their imports from Canada. Canada could not go on much longer financing that trade with loans and credits. The use of trade and exchange restrictions was widespread. At the time it looked to Canada as if fundamental changes would be required in its trade links and hence in trade policy.

For its part the United States had emerged as leader of the free world. It had just introduced the Marshall Plan to help European reconstruction and was feeling secure and strong enough to indulge in a generous view of its trade relations with its good neighbor Canada. It would be willing to tolerate the retention of the trade and exchange restrictions imposed by Canada for balance of payments reasons as a transitional arrangement while Canada was adapting its economy to the conditions of free trade. There would of course be some exceptions for critical products on both sides. All this could be carried out within the framework of GATT rules so that relations with other trading partners would not be adversely affected.

Despite these compelling reasons to make an agreement and U.S. willingness to accept transitional safeguards sensitive to Canadian needs, the opportunity was rejected. Was it just bad timing because of the difficult problems facing a prime minister about to retire, or were there deeper economic or political reasons for the failure? I will come back to these questions later.

I turn now to the automotive agreement, the best known and perhaps the most significant example of the sectoral free-trade option in the Canadian-U.S. trade relationship. Before the auto pact the Canadian automotive industry was archetypal of Canadian manufacturing. It was characterized by substantial protection; relatively small-scale, low-volume branch plants; and extensive product differentiation. It offered its products to the Canadian public and to certain Commonwealth markets at some 15 percent to 20 percent above U.S. prices. The techniques of protection were rather complex, embracing minimum Commonwealth content, duty differentials for classes of components and end-use items, preferential markets, drawbacks, and other devices. The complexity of the protective regime reflected the traditional paradox of Canadian tariff policy: how to maximize production and employment in Canada without imposing prices on the consumer that, compared with prices readily observable south of the border, were above politically acceptable limits.

In the late 1950s and early 1960s the Canadian auto industry found itself plagued by intensive international competition and a reduced capability for meeting it because of rapid technological change. To keep up with the new technology—automatic transmissions, for example—required capital investment of a size and scale simply beyond the economics of a truncated, small-scale industry producing mainly for a protected home market. The survival of the industry required either restructuring or a massive increase in protection.

Typically, the Canadian response was to do a little of both. In 1962 Canada introduced a duty remission scheme for imported transmissions and engines on a dollar-for-dollar basis equivalent to any increase achieved in exporting Canadian-made components. In 1963 the scheme was broadened to grant a duty remission on any vehicle or component import if matched by equivalent exports of vehicles or parts. In essence the scheme was designed to encourage increased specialization, larger production runs, and reduced costs through expanding exports.

In response to complaints by its domestic auto parts producers, the United States launched an investigation under its countervailing duty law to determine whether the Canadian measure consisted of a "bounty or grant." Canada argued that its measure expanded trade and was not restrictive. The review was never completed because both countries were sufficiently concerned about the impact that an adverse ruling would have on overall trade and other relations to compel them to seek a more constructive answer.

After intensive negotiations, the Automotive Products Trade Agreement was forged. Broadly speaking, the agreement provided for free trade between the two countries in all original equipment parts and vehicles. Replacement parts, tires, batteries, and used cars were not included. A number of important safeguards were written into the agreement, and certain undertakings were given to the Canadian government by the motor vehicle manufacturers with respect to their production plans. Essentially the conditions of the agreement were designed to ensure Canada an orderly transition as its auto industry adapted itself to the challenging condition of free trade with the United States.

The agreement was unlimited in duration but subject to termination on one year's notice by either party. U.S. insistence on a three-year limit for the safeguards was resisted; in its place the agreement provided for a comprehensive review in 1968. The agreement has now been in force with only minor changes for almost two decades. Reviews have been held, but the safeguards remain in place, although in the main they are no longer operational.

Over the life of the agreement there have been complaints from both sides, depending principally on how the balance of trade fluctuated from period to period. The U.S. side has argued that the safeguards were meant to disappear after a transitional period. For its part Canada has argued that the safeguards are needed as a safety net to ensure that its industry could participate on a fair and equitable basis in an expanding North American market.

Although the auto pact has not solved (nor could it) all the actual or perceived problems in the Canadian automotive industry, it has been generally successful. Its adaptation to changing circumstances has been slow in coming, however. The major challenges of Japanese competition and changing consumer tastes in recent years have inevitably created stresses and strains that intensified the need for updating the pact. Failure to do so has not been a fatal blow, however; the auto pact is very much operational.

Allow me a quick reference to the impact of GATT Tokyo round tariff negotiations on the Canadian-U.S. free-trade issue. When Canada completes the implementation of Tokyo round tariff concessions in 1987, the average rate of duty on dutiable imports will be 9 percent to 10 percent, although this embraces a number of rates that are substantially higher. The Tokyo round provided no significant additions to the free list. After Tokyo round concessions are fully in place, the average U.S. tariff on dutiable goods will be about 5.5 percent. This average obscures some much higher rates on certain major products of interest to Canada, including petrochemicals, rolling stock, and a range of textiles and clothing. Nonetheless it is fair to say that nontariff measures and the U.S. system of contingency protection—antidumping regulations, countervailing duties, and emergency import measures—constitute more formidable constraints to Canadian exports and investment in Canada than do tariffs.

Conclusions from U.S.-Canadian trade history

The lessons that emerge from the history of Canadian-U.S. trade relations may help us to understand the reciprocity or free-trade issue.

First, the massive and rich U.S. market has had an irresistible allure for Canada that finds expression in recurrent interest on the part of many Canadians in seeking reciprocal free trade. Canadians have thus instinctively recognized a fundamental truth about their economic affairs, namely that an open trade door to the U.S. market can help overcome some of the fundamental weaknesses of a small, widely dispersed home market. Canadians have not needed the help of economists and researchers to reach this conclusion.

At the same time, the United States has been largely indifferent to the idea of reciprocal free trade with Canada, and for equally good material reasons. With its vast home market and much smaller dependence on trade, there is much less advantage in free trade for the United States in immediate economic terms. U.S. interest in free trade with Canada has usually been inspired by considerations not confined to a search for gains in trade.

Canadian interest in reciprocity traditionally has peaked during periods of economic difficulty or when Canada has been frustrated by difficulties with other trading partners, particularly the United Kingdom and Western Europe. The United States, by contrast, traditionally has turned inward and reverted to more protectionist policies in the face of hard times. Thus there has been a recurrent mismatch of goals and interests in matters of trade policy.

The National Policy of tariff protection, a critical turning point in Canadian commercial affairs, was in no small measure a reaction to indifference on the part of the United States to the Canadian search for closer trade relations. Protection then led to the creation of strong domestic special interest groups that draped themselves in the domestic flag of nationalism or the imperial flag of the Commonwealth to resist and defeat the export-oriented sectors of the economy that yearned for free trade with the United States.

Despite the restrictive policies sometimes adopted by Canada and more often by the United States, however, the strong natural economic forces that flow from sharing a continent have asserted themselves. Trade between Canada and the United States has achieved a higher level of mutually advantageous exchange than takes place between any two other countries.

Periodic efforts by Canada to break out of its small domestic market and solve its trade dilemma by seeking options abroad—imperial preferences, the Diefenbaker trade diversion, the Sharp third option, interest in the Pacific Rim—have all met with very little success because there was an insufficient economic foundation to build upon. There simply has been no viable alternative to the U.S. market.

Free trade and economics
In developing this presentation I have not discussed the economic consequences of the tariff. This is not an oversight. There are few subjects of economic policy in the world context or in the context of Canada that have been examined more frequently or more thoroughly. The conclusions are clear and unequivocal. Except for a few dissenters who for reasons of special pleading, narrow self-interest, or just plain ignorance will argue otherwise, investigators agree that for advanced industrial countries like the United States and Canada protection is costly in real economic terms and that removing protection yields economic benefits. If there continues to be legitimate economic debate about this matter, it focuses on the size of the gains or losses, the short-term and longer-term impact of reduced protection, and the costs of adjustment to policy changes. Much more important aspects of the general debate relate to such noneconomic considerations as national objectives in the social, cultural, and political realms that often go beyond questions of income and wealth.

If we can accept the basic thesis that real economic gains can be achieved by the removal of protection, how great are these gains? Is the game worth the candle? Again, this subject has been worked over rather extensively for Canada, especially in recent years.

No one can say for certain precisely what would be the consequences for Canada of a full free-trade arrangement with the United States, but based on reliable studies by competent professionals, we can say that after the initial adjustments have been made the gains would be large. Major restructuring would occur in manufacturing, as it did in the automotive industry following the free-trade agreement. But other sectors as well, including agriculture, primary resource processing, and business services, can also make significant gains. There is currently about a 25 percent differential in per capita income between Canada and the United States. The causes for this substantial difference are deeply rooted in differences in geography, population, and stage of economic development. But protection is not an insignificant reason for lower per capita incomes in Canada. Perhaps 10 of the 25 percentage points could be removed over time if Canada had unqualified access to the U.S. market as part of a free-trade arrangement. Even if the gain were only half that, real output per year would increase by $20 billion.

What of the United States? Here too the answer is unequivocal. Worthwhile economic gains can be made by the removal of protection. But the much larger size of the U.S. economy, its huge domestic market, and its much smaller dependence on foreign trade ensure that in relative terms the economic gains for the United States would be smaller than for Canada.

Indeed, if one looked at trade gains alone it would be hard to raise much enthusiasm in the United States for the free-trade option. But there are advantages, albeit less tangible, in such an arrangement. Not least of these would be the removal of recurrent grievances on both sides of the border that constantly threaten to sour relationships in related economic and noneconomic spheres. For example, some recent manifestations of nationalism in Canada, particularly in the review of foreign investment proposals and in complaints about the behavior of nonresident-controlled corporations have their origin in Canadian frustration over the inadequacies of trade relations with the United States. If we can solve the trade issue, we can go a long way toward solving the investment issue as well.

Suggestions for a free-trade agreement

Whether Canadians like it or not, the hard truth is that the only real options available to them are to continue along the present path of incremental improvements under GATT or to try to reach a bilateral arrangement with the United States for partial or total free trade. The emergence of trade blocs, the relentless sweep of new technology, and the limited negotiating scope left for Canada at present tariff levels suggest that simply retaining the status quo will become increasingly difficult if we are to enjoy economic growth and improved standards of living. The option of closer relations with the United States, even if the United States were willing, has of course high risks of its own. A great deal would depend on what kind of an agreement Canada could negotiate.

I would like to turn now to consideration of these risks, actual and perceived, and to see how far they can reasonably be overcome or reduced by the negotiating process or perhaps by designing new approaches. My main emphasis will be on the economic risks, but I will occasionally venture into the political field as well.

The observations offered here apply to a free-trade arrangement that would meet the requirements of GATT, that is, it would apply to substantially all trade between the two countries. This does not of course mean that there would be no room for a few exceptions on both sides. Most of the points relevant to a comprehensive approach would also apply to a sectoral trade approach. Apparently, however, political concerns are less significant if the approach taken were to be by trade sectors.

The objection raised most often on the Canadian side is that most manufacturing industries are structured to serve a much smaller market and therefore do not have the plant, equipment, personnel, management experience, or connections to withstand an unprotected onslaught from abroad or to derive benefits from reaching into the larger market. This is a valid argument. Many cases can be cited in which these conditions prevail. There may also be a few cases in which a similar objection may be raised by U.S. industry. The logical approach to this problem would be to design the agreement so as to include reasonable transitional measures that would give the weaker partner the opportunity to upgrade his capacity. The stronger partner would have to be willing to open his market more quickly. Needless to say, such special treatment would have to be truly transitional. Adjustment assistance for both capital and labor might also be necessary. Such assistance was built into the regime following the auto pact and enjoyed a good reception and a considerable measure of success.

A second objection is that some industries are so far behind that they simply could not muster the resources, human and material, to compete in a free market. Such cases are likely to occur in industries that are not growing and would therefore be a poor risk for substantial new investment. No doubt there are a few of these industries on both sides of the border. They are in decline and nothing much can be done for them, although there may be room for some help to encourage them into new lines of endeavor. Such new opportunities are likely to be greater in an environment of change where new markets are being opened up under the free-trade program. But it will not be possible to help everyone, simply by reason of lack of resources. Thus not all painful change can be avoided or compensated for. Here again the availability of a period of transition will help mitigate the damage to individual companies and workers.

A third objection is that many Canadian enterprises were established in Canada in order to get behind the tariff wall, that they are owned and controlled by nonresidents, and that their reason for locating in Canada would disappear with the dismantling of the tariff. They would simply pick up and go, choosing to serve the Canadian market from their home bases. In those instances in which the investment in Canada is small or antiquated, such results might indeed occur. In other cases, long experience with Canadian operations and the new opportunities in the U.S. market would encourage companies not only to stay but to grow. Nonetheless there would be substantial adjustments and rearrangements within industries: specialization on fewer products, exclusive licensing agreements, and perhaps mergers or takeovers. The benefits from free trade would occur precisely because this rationalization was taking place. It would be best to acknowledge that change is not only inevitable but is to be welcomed and encouraged.

Another objection is that even where new trading opportunities might suggest locating in Canada, uncertainty about the permanence of the arrangements would favor locating in the larger of the two markets unless the advantages of Canada were overwhelming. This is not likely to be the condition for most manufacturing industries. As an argument it applies not only to foreign-owned enterprises but also to domestic-owned companies and to potential new investors from Canada and abroad. Yet this is one of the most difficult objections to meet. To the extent that permanence can be built into the new system by treaty or other means, the worry would be eased but would not disappear. A suggestion will be offered later to help resolve this and related problems.

Still another objection to a free-trade agreement is that it would be dangerous to embark on major new investments geared to the U.S. market in the face of actual or potential nontariff barriers and actual or potential contingency protection, such as antidumping regulations, countervailing measures, or other emergency import restrictions. This is not a hollow concern. Canadian businessmen can cite chapter and verse to verify its validity.

During my experience on boards of directors in the private sector, I have encountered several instances in which decisions about where to locate a new plant have been taken on exactly these grounds—or else for the purpose of taking advantage of Buy American or similar kinds of protective measures. It may be that the U.S. negotiators can cite cases that work the other way. In practice, however, when locational decisions are made contrary to strict market considerations, it is not unreasonable to expect that the larger market will be favored as a safer haven.

To deal with this family of problems, the free-trade agreement must have a clear commitment from both countries that they will apply full national treatment to the services, products, and enterprises of the other, that is, treatment identical to that accorded domestic goods and domestic-owned enterprises. To be absolutely certain, I would insist that national treatment apply not only to trade but to investment as well.

But even with such provisions there remains the danger of abrogation of the agreement itself, with large potential losses for investments dependent on the U.S. market. This problem is identical to one discussed earlier.

A final and all-encompassing objection is that the disruption to enterprises, plants, and personnel brought on by free trade will be so extensive and costly as to overshadow for a long time the economic benefits to be anticipated from the new trade opportunities. No one can predict just how extensive the adjustments would have to be, but it would be wise to expect that in some industries at least, the required changes will be of major proportions. Transitional arrangements, adjustment assistance, and on rare occasions a decent burial may be required.

In the review of the history of Canadian-U.S. trade relations from colonial days to the present and in the analysis of Canadian fears about the economic dangers of free trade with the United States, one clear and consistent theme emerges. There is an ever-present danger that a sudden shift in U.S. trade policy directed either to the total relationship or to particular trade sectors could severely affect Canada's total economy or could so damage the market for particular products as to render a capital investment worthless.

While it is true that one cannot cite recent examples of U.S. changes in trade policy comparable to the abrogation of the 1854 Reciprocity Agreement or the introduction of the Hawley-Smoot tariff, one can recall the Connally surcharges of August 1971 and the threats at the Smithsonian meetings later that year to terminate the automotive agreement if Canada refused to conform to U.S. ideas as to what an appropriate exchange rate policy for Canada might be. There are also a number of examples of actual or threatened restrictive trade measures affecting Canadian exports and investment in more recent years. In this context it is important to observe that the actual imposition of trade restrictions is not necessarily the most serious aspect of the problem. The threat posed by an investigation under, say, the countervailing duty law or even an obscure proposal in the Congress that will likely never see the light of day may be sufficient to serve as an effective deterrent to investment in Canada. The dog need not bite. He need only bark now and then to do the damage.

I can provide examples from my experience in government and in business to demonstrate that this ever-present fear has affected key investment decisions that have been very costly to Canadian economic development. The beneficiary has almost always been the United States because given the relative size of markets the prudent course is to locate on the safe side of the border. It goes without saying that uncertainty in commercial policy becomes more serious in a free-trade framework in which Canadian industry is expected to restructure in order to serve the U.S. market. To the extent that sensible investment decisions are inhibited by this fear, the benefits for Canada from free trade would be diminished or perhaps wiped out.

There is no easy answer to this kind of problem. Only a long and consistent record of abstinence by the United States can overcome it. And we are a long way from that.

Reluctance to accept this pessimistic conclusion has led me to suggest several features of a free-trade arrangement that might help. The principal one, which I referred to earlier, would require both countries to apply unqualified national treatment to the goods, services, and enterprises of the other. Such a provision, supported by the full weight of a formal treaty with very strict limits on abrogation, would go a considerable distance to ensure stability of the commercial policy arrangements. But would it go far enough? Probably not.

I would like to suggest another possible approach, one rather novel and unorthodox, but worth thought. I put it forward in broad outline with all due diffidence and modesty. It would be as follows:

—As part of the Canadian-U.S. free-trade arrangement a trade disruption insurance program would be established. Initial funds would be provided by the two governments in proportion to the export trade of each country covered by the trade agreement. Whether by cash or by guarantee the fund would have to be large enough to be credible.

—Coverage would be available to any U.S. or Canadian business engaged in exporting goods or services to the other and be sufficient to protect a substantial proportion of the investment at risk.

—The insurance premium would be large enough to be meaningful but not so expensive as to be prohibitive. Premiums would be adjusted after several years of practical experience with the program.

—Claims would be made on the basis of actual damage caused by a trade restriction imposed by one of the participating governments in contravention of the agreement. Escape clause action would be treated as a contravention. Claims would have to include proof of damage.

—The insurance institution would be governed by a board of directors made up of an equal number of members from each government and a chairman acceptable to both. All decisions of the board with respect to claims would be binding and final.

—If the insurance fund were to require replenishment at any time, the two governments would contribute additional funds in proportion to the damage claims awarded arising out of restrictive measures imposed by the two governments. If one of the two governments had not taken restrictive action, it would not be required to make additional contributions.

—Dividends would be paid to the participating governments if the fund grew beyond some fixed level. Such surpluses could signal that premiums be reduced.

A program of this kind would go a long way toward removing fears about commercial policy instability that inhibit investment and trade. It is put forward on the assumption that actual restrictive measures would be infrequent, an assumption not inconsistent with recent experience. Because a trade restriction would be costly, the obligation to replenish the fund would itself serve as a deterrent to its use.

If the United States and Canada were able to work out a free-trade agreement, it would be a good thing for both countries and a good example to the world. It would make both countries richer. It would also make us better neighbors, because it would remove many of the issues about which we have been squabbling for many years.

A free-trade arrangement would not weaken Canadian sovereignty or Canadian resolve to remain independent. Indeed, by enriching Canada and by raising its confidence, the agreement would strengthen Canada's purpose and its ability to survive as a strong free nation.

If these conclusions are valid, may we expect early progress to establish free trade between the United States and Canada? I do not think it will happen, certainly not now. Conditions are not bad enough in Canada nor are they good enough in the United States to provide just the right mixture required to ignite the political leaders on both sides of the border. That is what history tells us, and history is usually right.

Reducing Nontariff Barriers

MYER RASHISH

I HAVE a simple message and a simple proposition to offer. It is that Canada and the United States are now in a phase of bilateral relations, a juncture, so to speak, that offers some interesting possibilities for putting trade and investment relations—the two are functionally related—on a surer footing. This juncture reflects a convergence of interests on the part of both countries that ought to be exploited.

What does this mutual interest consist of? On the Canadian side, as reflected in the Department of External Affairs' report, *Canadian Trade Policy for the 1980s,* and in the sectoral free-trade initiative, there seems to be a growing interest in securing access and maintaining a greater assurance of access to the U.S. market. Canada has become, in fact, increasingly dependent on the U.S. market, and this has served Canada's interests. It has fostered investment and capital formation in industries capable of achieving sufficient economies of scale and levels of productivity that have made Canadian companies increasingly competitive in the U.S. market.

There is an increasing awareness of the importance of the U.S. market to Canada's economic development. The recent smart rate of U.S. growth has been reflected in a 15 percent growth in Canadian exports to the United States in 1983 as well as a $12 billion bilateral trade surplus.

But, as Sigmund Freud told us, increased dependence carries with it increased risks, and increased risks provoke greater anxiety. Canada, understandably, is anxious about its capacity to maintain its access to the U.S. market and to avoid the kinds of policy decisions, whether taken by the U.S. executive or legislature, that would introduce a high degree of uncertainty in Canada's capacity to sell. This uncertainty would tend to dampen the interest in investment in Canada and thereby reduce the capacity of Canadian industry to reach levels of output and productivity that would be sustainable. Thus we have on the Canadian side a growing interest in security of access to the U.S. market.

On the American side, there seems to be a receptive attitude toward initiatives for improving trade relations with Canada. To some extent this attitude has less to do with economic benefits that would accrue to the United States directly from the bilateral relationship and more to do with the larger environment in which trade policy is conducted. The United States has proposed a number of initiatives in trade policy. But a General Agreement on Tariffs and Trade (GATT) ministerial meeting in November 1982 failed to produce very much in the way of positive results. The United States has also had a rather bitter running debate with the Japanese over trade policy. The European Community does not appear to be very helpful; it seems that we have nobody to talk to there. Then Canada suggested that we get together and talk about sectoral free trade. Instead of stirring the pot of protectionism, we have been given an opportunity to bake a new cake together. It is very appealing. And the response of the United States has been favorable—inconclusive to be sure, but favorable.

Functional-sector vs. product-sector approach

How do we take advantage of this coincidence of interests? My message is that the Canadian proposal for free trade in limited product sectors is neither a particularly effective way of solving Canada's problems nor does it engage sufficiently the interest of the United States in doing something positive with Canada. I have an alternative to offer. Instead of free trade in product sectors, we ought to consider a functional-sector approach.

A functional-sector approach would focus on the nontariff barrier issues on which substantial progress was made during the Tokyo round of GATT negotiations. The product-sector approach proposed in the Canadian initiative is, after all, not aimed at free trade in the conventional sense of removing tariffs. Tariffs by and large are inconsequential. When the reductions negotiated in the Tokyo round are fully in force in 1987, 80 percent of Canada's exports to the United States will be free of duty, and about two-thirds of U.S. exports to Canada will enter free of duty.

Canada's product-sector initiative therefore is not aimed mainly at reducing tariffs, even though there are a few industries such as petrochemicals and textiles and apparel for which U.S. tariffs are still important. The initiative is rather, it seems to me, aimed at trying, within the product sector, to get an agreement—which would have to be, of course, reciprocated in some form by Canada—to limit the freedom that the United States government might exercise with respect to Canadian imports. In other words, the goal is to reduce as much as possible Washington's flexibility, if you will, in applying various types of restraints against imports from Canada.

If that is the real interest on the part of Canada, then a product-sector approach—even if it were successful in these terms— would at most accomplish this objective only with respect to a handful of product sectors. There are only three or four now under serious consideration, and one wonders whether the game would be worth the candle. To be able to get guarantees against Buy American rules or guarantees against the application of safeguard measures with respect to iron and steel and two or three more of the sectors under consideration seems a small gain.

Instead, Canada should be interested in obtaining those kinds of guarantees on a wide variety of nontariff measures that apply to all its exports to the United States and not only to those covered by a product-sector arrangement. In short, the functional-sector approach, which would involve reaching a deal on Buy American rules or on safeguards or, if possible, on antidumping and countervailing measures, would have to address the very same issues as the product-sector approach but in a manner that might produce substantial benefits.

Furthermore, I accept as given that political constraints in Canada mean the notion of a free-trade area with the United States is not in the cards, certainly not in the near term. Because of the emotion free trade evokes north of the border, it is largely a symbolic issue. The functional-sector approach avoids that particular problem.

In any event, the problems of trade relations today and in the future are not going to center on tariffs. They will have to do with domestic policies in the participating countries, whether on a multilateral basis or in terms of bilateral trade. We are close to bilateral tariff-free trade already, or will be by the time the Tokyo round tariff reductions are in place. The issues for the future are largely in the nontariff area. We have to begin to address these more complicated and difficult issues that basically involve extensions of domestic policy.

Furthermore, a functional-sector approach in a bilateral agreement between Canada and the United States has the advantage of largely avoiding problems with GATT. In contrast, anything done in product sectors is bound to be in violation of GATT. We would have to get a GATT waiver because unless we negotiated complete free trade with minimal derogations, sectoral arrangements would be in violation of Article 24.

The functional-sector approach can, moreover, serve as a

reasonable model for what might come later in GATT negotiations. The agenda that the United States has put on the table for the next round of negotiations, whenever that takes place—revision of the safeguard clause, reducing barriers to trade in services, and so on—consists of many of the same items to be covered by an arrangement between Canada and the United States. One could in fact conceive of a Canadian-U.S. functional-sector arrangement as a model for a larger, multilateral arrangement to be negotiated in GATT.

There is, after all, in the Tokyo round nontariff barrier agreements the principle of conditional most-favored-nation treatment. The Government Procurement Code, for example, does not apply to all parties, only to those that subscribe to its terms. We would have a kind of variant of conditional most-favored-nation treatment between Canada and the United States by dealing with nontariff issues in a way that could offer a model for a larger multilateral agreement on the same issues.

Then, too, a product-sector arrangement could well run into very serious political problems in the United States. It would have to be implemented by an act of Congress, and the minute one begins to deal with product sectors and with industry or subindustry groups, the attention of the industries concerned is focused on the specific provisions of the agreement. It quickly becomes parochial and politicized, with every jot and tittle being examined very closely. The steel industry, for example, is going to inspect any product-sector agreement on steel in minute detail. With a functional approach, on the other hand—and the Tokyo round results are a precedent—the subjects at issue, at least on the surface, are unrelated to the specific interests of any particular industry.

Obviously, an industry group that happens to be interested in the problems of subsidization by foreign suppliers will look carefully at what is done with respect to any agreement on countervailing duties. But that would not be specifically a steel agreement. It would be a countervailing duty agreement and therefore would be a bit more immune to parochial political pressures.

Finally, everything with respect to tariffs that can be done in a product-sector agreement can be done in a functional-sector agreement. If we want to reach agreement on duties in some particular sector on a balanced basis between the two countries, that can be included.

Under section 151 of the 1974 act, which still applies, the results of this agreement would go back to the Congress for an up or down vote, with no amendments, a privileged rule, and all the rest, just as the results of the Tokyo round were put to the Congress.

Given that the initiative for product-sector free trade has been under discussion and that there seems to be some interest and goodwill on both sides, we should, as Sam Rayburn used to say, strike a blow for freedom. We should make sure that the blow we strike is as resounding as possible. The product-sector approach is of limited utility. By trying a functional-sector approach instead, we stand to gain much more tangible benefits.

General Discussion

CHARLES PERRAULT of Perconsult Ltd., commented that Canada is entering a new and more difficult trading environment. Formerly its favorable position in natural resources provided trading advantages, but now it will have to be more competitive in areas in which it has traditionally found difficulty. The United States faces similar problems.

Public perception of this problem is not yet very great. Nevertheless, there seems to be a growing concern that Canada is approaching an extraordinarily difficult period from a competitive point of view. This period may afford the political opportunity to develop a larger free-trade area with the United States. Unless people are hurt, they are not going to be very farsighted. They probably have not yet been hurt enough. However, the level of injury might increase rapidly enough in Canada that politicians could exert the necessary leadership to move forward.

Reisman responded that Canadians did indeed look for alternatives that involved reaching out, particularly to the U.S. market, when things were bad in Canada. He hoped Perrault was wrong in predicting that conditions would worsen and added that if he was not, then perhaps Canadians would be driven by the devil if not by good sense.

Barbara Jacob of the European Communities delegation to the United States said she was particularly interested to hear that the chief Canadian negotiator of the Automotive Parts Agreement now advocated a general free-trade agreement. The bilateral Automotive Parts Agreement had required a waiver by GATT, which was granted in 1965. She asked Reisman whether the current Canadian-U.S. approach toward new sectoral agreements would in current circumstances receive a similar waiver from GATT.

Reisman said that nothing in his remarks should be taken to imply that he thought the automotive agreement was a failure. It is very much alive, it is working reasonably well, and it has done a great deal for Canada and for the United States. It did not solve all the problems, however, and it gave rise to a good deal of friction, some of which is still present. He estimated that because of the rationalization of the Canadian automotive industry, the agreement resulted in cumulative savings to Canada in excess of $22 billion. He had no estimate for savings in the United States. Nonetheless, he was more interested in a free-trade arrangement because he considered the present a time for boldness. He was also no longer an official and therefore more prone to be contaminated by an academic and scholarly atmosphere and to try to reach out a little further. Rashish's approach brought him back to real-life struggles at the negotiating table and made a lot of sense.

In answer to the specific question, Reisman argued that the GATT aspect was not that vital. Canadians had never sought a waiver on the auto pact; they simply extended it worldwide. The United States did seek and get a waiver. If now a sectoral or functional or total agreement could be reached, he thought ways would be found to get GATT to accommodate it.

MacLaury rephrased the question. If instead of a bold initiative for free trade the two countries went for the sectoral-trade approach, would there not be more questions raised in GATT and less chance this time of getting a waiver than was the case in the auto agreement? He asked Reisman if sectoral-trade agreements could be drafted so as to pass muster.

Reisman replied that was so but that his problem with the sectoral approach was not GATT. Rather, he believed the sectoral approach was not imaginative enough; it would bring out all the narrowest trade interests, those that look for bilateral balances. It would not fire the imagination of the people needed to make these things work. He considered the sectoral approach too puny and not exciting enough.

Gary Horlick of O'Melveny and Myers thought Rashish's idea was attractive in that it could avoid some GATT problems. He asked Rashish on which nontariff barriers he would start, suggesting that subsidies might be put off to the last because consideration of countervailing duties would also have to be part of a negotiation.

Rashish replied that in Canada's interest he thought government procurement and safeguard measures; that is, various types of escape clauses would be the two principal candidates.

Sandy Vogelgesang of the U.S. embassy in Canada asked about the politics involved in the functional approach. She thought, for

example, that government procurement would raise serious political difficulties.

Rashish agreed that both approaches would have political
problems. No one wants to see the measure of protection or
advantage that he enjoys removed. The product-sector approach,
as Reisman noted, is simply inadequate. It is parochial. It invites
contests between manufacturers of widgets and the importers of
widgets. The functional-sector approach at least addresses a
broader problem and at first blush is not identified with any
particular product interest. Rashish also shared Reisman's view
that sometimes more imaginative proposals—he considered his
own proposal marginally more imaginative than a product-sector
approach—have a better chance of being accepted politically than
smaller, less imaginative proposals. He noted a kind of perverse
quantum mechanics at work in American politics. The mind of
the Congress and the public could be captured with ideas that
have some space and dimension to them, whereas small ideas
provoke resistance and parochial debate.

MacLaury asked Reisman to elaborate on the provisions of a
trade disruption insurance fund and any precedents for it.

Reisman said he had included the insurance idea in a set of
eighteen proposals he had presented a few years ago to a royal
commission investigation of the Canadian auto industry, but
nobody paid attention to the idea. He had revised it and thought
it now made more sense in the context of general rather than
sectoral free trade. For Canadians, the fund would ease worries
that new investments based on a free-trade regime would be
endangered if the United States suddenly decided to impose
restrictions. Canadians, he noted, like to think they would never
restrict trade in these circumstances. In any event, they would
think twice about doing so if they had to pay for it.

Isaiah Frank of the Johns Hopkins University asked whether a
functional agreement between Canada and the United States would
be open to adherence by any country willing to accept its
obligations. He thought it would have to be.

Rashish agreed that such a bilateral agreement would be a
model for a multilateral agreement.

Frank then commented that such functional agreements would
lose the political advantages sought from a closer Canadian-U.S.
economic relationship.

Rashish replied that the answer depended on the objective of
the exercise. If the Canadian objective was to ensure greater

security and confidence about access to the U.S. market, then a functional agreement would meet the need whether or not it would be open subsequently to other signatories as part of a multilateral agreement. Further, in such negotiations it would also be possible to address specific issues that have bearing only or primarily on the two countries. For example, in the case of government procurement a problem arises because of the difference in the authorities of the states and municipalities in the United States and the provinces of Canada. The provinces have a great deal more autonomy. They are not subject to a provision analogous to the commerce clause of the Constitution. It is possible to address that kind of an issue in the context of a bilateral agreement, but it might be irrelevant, by and large, to other countries. If nobody else is interested in subscribing to that particular provision, it will stand by itself.

Ernest Preeg of the Overseas Development Council thought that in the product-sector approach GATT would be a more significant problem for the United States than had been suggested and certainly would pose more difficulties than it did in achieving the automotive pact. At that time Canada did not ask for a waiver because any company able to meet criteria laid down in the agreement was eligible for treatment. The structure of the industry was such that only a few North American companies could qualify. The United States did ask for a GATT waiver and obtained it in the fairly favorable environment of the Kennedy round of negotiations. The United States was also able to argue that since it was importing and exporting almost identical vehicles there would be no effect on the price in the United States. There would be no disadvantage to competing exporters. These rather unique circumstances would not be repeated in new sectoral agreements. How could the United States argue that such agreements would be consistent with GATT?

Peter Morici of the National Planning Association pointed out that after the Tokyo round of cuts is completed, about 75 percent of Canadian-U.S. trade in industrial products will be free of tariffs. At that time, the average weighted tariff in the United States will be about 6 percent and in Canada about 9 percent. If sectoral agreements could be concluded for the major remaining high-tariff areas—textiles, for which the tariff rate will still average 25 percent; chemicals, for which it will average 15 percent; and possibly steel—90 to 95 percent of Canadian-U.S. industrial trade will be free of duty. If, then, the two countries eliminated their 2 percent tariffs, industrial trade between them would be substantially free. The hard part would be to complete three or four sectoral agreements at once. If it could be done, the GATT problem would disappear.

MacLaury asked Reisman why the auto agreement is not a model for sectoral free trade. Reisman said that the auto industry was one in which all the assemblers and a good number of the parts makers in Canada were U.S. companies. That is a quite different situation than exists in the industries now being considered. Reisman said he did not use the auto agreement as his model for the future because it does not fit the bill. The agreement has caused frictions and disagreements, partly because not enough has happened in the rest of industry and trade. The agreement had to be negotiated at that time and it was working well. It benefits both countries, but that model does not fire the imagination to envision where the two countries should go from here.

An Official Perspective

Canadian-U.S. Trade Negotiations: A Status Report

WILLIAM E. BROCK

TWO-WAY merchandise trade between Canada and the United States in 1983 was valued at more than $90 billion, a sum greater than U.S. trade with all ten members of the European Community. Nearly a fifth of our exports go to Canada and over two-thirds of Canadian exports come to the United States.

These magnitudes, if not the exact figures, are familiar to most people interested in the Canadian-U.S. relationship or in foreign trade policy. They tell us that things are generally going well and profitably for both countries so far as trade is concerned.

Bilateral possibilities

We are now in the process of looking at opportunities for removing some of the barriers to a further expansion of trade. In doing so, both sides recognize that without stretching the definition unduly we can be said already to have a free-trade zone. When the Tokyo round cuts are fully in force, about 65 percent of our goods will enter Canada duty free while about 80 percent of Canada's exports to the United States will similarly be duty free. Free-trade areas reviewed by GATT under Article 24 have ranged from 6.4 percent of all trade (the European Community with Tanzania, Uganda, and Kenya) to 93 percent (the United Kingdom and Ireland). Given the extent of duty-free trade between Canada and the United States, then, the present bilateral discussions amount to an examination of some of the exceptions to our de facto free-trade area.

A big step toward duty-free trade was taken almost twenty years ago in the automobile pact. We now have joint working groups reviewing steel, agricultural implements, traded computer services and other elements of the "informatics" sector, and government procurement issues with particular emphasis on urban mass transit.

We understand that the Canadian government is reviewing the petrochemical, textile and clothing, and red meat sectors. For our part, work is under way on a number of fronts, including forest products, cosmetics, furniture, and alcoholic beverages.

65

It is well to remind ourselves, however, that freedom from tariffs, even if that condition can be extended to more of our trade, does not ensure that restraints other than tariffs will not limit or impede the exchange of goods and services across our borders. Most of the world has been inching toward elimination of tariffs. At the same time, governments have proved to be marvellously sophisticated at devising nontariff ways of intervening in the market place. Perhaps we should think of paralleling our sectoral talks with a functional approach that could take in some of the nontariff barriers, actual or prospective.

In this connection, I can report that we already have reached an understanding with Canada on procedures to be followed when one of us invokes the GATT escape clause, Article 19, on any product of interest to the other. Article 19 has been in force for thirty-six years with little having been agreed about the interpretation to be placed on its far-from-crystal-clear paragraphs. During the Tokyo round a major effort to elaborate Article 19 into a new "safeguard clause" ended in failure. We tried again for multilateral agreement at the 1981 meeting of the GATT ministers, without success.

Now we have a bilateral accord in which we have spelled out what amounts to an extension of Article 19 for the United States and Canada. In particular, we have addressed directly and fully the question of the permissible response when one of the parties invokes the escape clause to impose a new restriction on imports. At least as far as the United States and Canada are concerned, the right of either party to receive compensation or to impose equivalent import restrictions is specifically defined in procedural and substantive terms.

The bilateral understanding is wholly consistent with GATT. It could in fact be a model for the other contracting parties to use as an interpretive protocol to Article 19. Even as bilateral agreements under the Trade Agreements Act of 1934 became the basis for the General Agreement of 1947, so perhaps will bilateral understandings show the way to some of the revisions and additions needed to make GATT a more effective instrument today.

Multilateral requirements
Nevertheless, we recognize the limitations of a bilateral approach. It is not that we could not come to an agreement that could qualify under the terms of GATT. Arguably, we could. It is rather that our exercise is in some respects a departure from the postwar pattern of multilateral negotiations, an aberration if you

will. For the past thirty-five years—since World War II and the disaster, to put it charitably, of the 1920s and 1930s—we have tried to move ahead comprehensively, recognizing that all genuine participants had to give as well as take but believing, correctly, that on balance there would be handsome net benefits for everyone. That approach is still the way, over a long period, to the ultimate goal of removing official restrictions on international trade.

This is not to say that whatever we may be able to do now will have to be a setback to progress. But we must not forget that the world stands in need of further rounds of negotiations to bring down trade barriers. Experience tells us that the best venue will be GATT and that the most rewarding results will come from as broad a negotiation as we can muster. In short, we should not think of our current effort as some kind of end-all for our trade relations.

Finally, as economic interdependence proceeds, we need to give more thought to our mutual exposure to the vicissitudes of macroeconomic policymaking. As we see now, particularly in our problems with Europe, divergent macroeconomic policies can cause, or be blamed for causing, distortions that can seem to translate themselves into stagnation and unemployment or into inflationary pressures. It is fair to say that present mechanisms for macroeconomic policy coordination are primitive. Beyond that, the adjustment mechanisms that come into play when policies diverge too much are not so much primitive as slow working.

I think that we have here one of the more sensitive aspects of international economic relations, and one that is destined to become more so. If we could come to grips with it more effectively between our two countries, the experience and example could be of great importance. But at the moment, that can only be a hope, not an expectation.

General Discussion

JOHN CURTIS of the Institute for Research on Public Policy in Ottawa asked Ambassador Brock for his views about the direction of U.S. trade policy—whether it will be primarily bilateral or multilateral in character. He referred to U.S. discussions with Canada, Israel, and the Association of Southeast Asian Nations and to the special trade relationship with the Caribbean. He asked whether these developments represented a fundamental shift in U.S. policy toward bilateralism. Or could they be, in part at least, intended to tell the Japanese and Europeans that the United States has alternatives if they are unwilling to help stop the erosion of the multilateral trading system?

Brock replied that the issues involved are complex. He stressed first that the multilateral system has worked magnificently over the past three decades and that the volume and scope of world trade would be smaller and narrower if it were not for GATT and the other postwar multilateral institutions—the International Monetary Fund and the World Bank. Yet we have in part exhausted a good deal of the system's genius for growth unless it is changed. For example, the growth of world trade will increasingly be in services rather than goods, and yet we have virtually no multilateral rules governing the exchange of services. If the system is to enable trade to grow in new areas as well as old, its negotiating coverage must be extended.

Second, we are near the end of the road in negotiating reductions in tariffs, and we must do a better job of negotiating reductions in nontariff barriers. We started that in Tokyo, but very few of the developing countries have signed any of the nontariff codes. Those that have done so were forced to by U.S. law on subsidies and countervailing duties. We do not have a pervasive, comprehensive system to reduce the impact of nontariff barriers.

Third, the multilateral system really exists for the defense of the small, not the large. The United States probably does not need a system. It is so big and so powerful that it can be above the rules. The only protection that the small nations have against the United States is an agreed-upon contract, such as GATT, that has dispute settlement procedures built in that are arguably enforceable or have the potential for being enforced. Unfortunately, the dispute settlement mechanism of GATT is not working very well. Neither is the antisubsidy mechanism, largely because of a dispute among developed countries. We need to make some progress in these matters or the system itself will be jeopardized.

Brock noted that when the trading system was put together after World War II, the United States, among others, objected to making it too comprehensive. It did not like the idea of an international trade organization. The United States argued, as did others, that the undertaking should be limited to trade in goods. That left us with GATT. Now we find that the system is inadequate because it does not cover services and other things.

Also, the countries that put together the trading system were basically market economy countries. That is no longer true. The eighty-eight members of GATT by and large are not pure market economies and have little prospect of becoming so. That being the case, it seems likely that decisions will increasingly be made on a political rather than an economic basis. And in that circumstance we must remember a fundamental rule of politics: there must be a system of rewards and penalties. Without that we may not be able to move very far.

We must develop new rewards and penalties. Not that we have a right to impose our will on anybody. We do not. And if we try, it will not work. But as the premier market in the world the United States has the capacity to offer an incentive, to say in effect, "If you are willing to live by a higher set of standards and to operate on a quid pro quo basis, there can be some tangible benefits to be derived therefrom."

If we do not do something along those lines, we will forfeit our leadership, and there will be no trading system. In other words, we have to provide some additional strength and leadership to the international trading system, and we have to do it by something more than rhetoric. Words do not mean much unless there is some tangible means of persuasion to back them up. Moreover if we offer incentives, we had better be prepared to have them accepted. This is an evolving process by which the United States would be willing to open itself to competition in an exchange from which we expect to derive benefits. If the rules do not profit both parties, they will not last.

Brock added that the United States would talk to Canada if the Canadians wish. We will talk to Israel, as they wish. And we will talk with others, perhaps. Then the members of the world system may begin to realize that there is net value in the reduction of barriers, and we can move matters forward.

Maurice Strong, chairman of the Canada Development Investment Corporation, said that the steam is almost out of the strong post–World War II drive toward multilateralism—most of it having been concentrated on tariffs—and that we really do need to take a look at the whole range of more sophisticated types of protectionism that are now on the horizon. To relate this to the Canadian-U.S. situation, he went on, some reasonably optimistic views have been offered by some old pros about the benefits to be derived from greater free trade between Canada and the United States. He suggested that the political impetus for greater Canadian-U.S. integration may well come from a factor that few might wish to subscribe to, and that is a mutual unwillingness to face the much more competitive world situation that now is developing.

While rhetoric is still officially very much in favor of the further evolution of multilateralism, many of the real political impulses in our societies come from a reluctance to face squarely the competitive rigors that are already forcing accommodations in some of our traditional industries. The impetus for closer integration may come from our combined need to confront a tough competitive world and to accept the adjustments in our economies that that competitive world will require.

Brock commented that Strong had touched on an important point. The tendency in the United States is to complain that it is at a disadvantage, that everybody in the world is targeting it. This he characterized as baloney. Our manufacturers, he noted, have the richest market in the world as their economic base. If it is not possible to build on that market and compete in Ghana or Japan or anywhere, something is wrong. We should not feel sorry for ourselves because we are everybody's export target. We are well off; that is true. But that gives us an economic advantage, not a disadvantage.

Of course one of the incentives for talking bilaterally is that a healthier North American industrial base will give us the tools with which to be more competitive globally. That statement is not to be taken in a defensive sense, because that would imply that we want to put up protectionist barriers. Actually, in talking about sectoral trade agreements we are talking about reducing barriers between us, not increasing barriers against anybody else. Both countries will be healthier as we move toward a reduction of barriers, but by no description can this be taken as an exercise to increase protection against somebody across the ocean. It would be a terrible mistake to do that.

Jack Warren, vice-chairman of the Bank of Montreal, noted that earlier speakers had felt that to approach liberalization by encouraging free trade in product sectors was lacking in imagination and would not be sufficiently beneficial. The approach should be larger by one means or another. He asked Brock to comment on the extent to which he believed the two executive authorities would be prepared to contemplate an enriched package and whether an enriched package between the United States and Canada, perhaps along the lines of a mixture of functional and product-sector areas, would be negotiable with the Congress.

Brock replied that the United States would be willing to consider anything that the Canadian government would like to do at whatever pace Canada chooses. It was his own feeling that as the larger partner in the exercise, the United States has to be particularly sensitive to the mood and the circumstances and the politics within Canada. That means that it must let Canada pretty well set the pace.

If it is in Canada's interest and in the interest of the United States, there will be a deal. If it is not in Canada's interest, then it certainly is of no value for the United States to push it because it will not work. The U.S. government would be prepared to match the Canadian government stride for stride as effectively as it can and as broadly as the Canadians wish. A broadened approach no doubt would offer greater economic opportunity for both sides in a shorter time, but that is talking pure economics. We do not live in a purely economic world. We live in a political world. Thus it is necessary to accept the judgment of the government of Canada as to what it thinks best for the people it represents. The United States will accept that judgment and be as supportive as it can. America does not want to create problems.

As for the Congress, the people there would like something positive to talk about in trade. They are getting fed up with the negative side as they continue to hear about the Wine Equity Act, the steel quota bill, domestic content, and so on. We have stopped shooting ourselves in the foot with a rifle; we now use a shotgun. Congress is tired of it; the members want to look at something more affirmative. They might well like to hear about a positive approach to trade.

Reisman referred to Brock's comment about the relationship between trade initiatives and macroeconomic policies in the two countries. He thought that when coordinating macroeconomic policies between the two countries is considered, it really means that Canada must adjust to the policies of the United States. It will not be the other way, given the relative weights of the two economies. Reisman suggested that in a world of floating exchange rates—assuming that countries are willing to let them float in response to differences in macroeconomic policy—there is no need to integrate or coordinate macroeconomic policies. To be sure, Canada is resisting any violent movement in the exchange rate because of fears of inflation and also because at least some of the authorities want to use the discipline of a more evenly regulated exchange rate to force appropriate adjustments in fiscal policy. But that is a domestic concern. Taking into account floating rates, is coordination and integration of macroeconomic policy necessary?

Brock accepted the premise that floating rates will, over a period of time, allow economic systems to match and merge even with different macroeconomic policies, because differences in macroeconomic policy will be reflected in exchange rates and this becomes an offsetting force. Moreover, he thought that Americans and Canadians should be cautious in talking about possibilities for coordinated macroeconomic policy. The United States does not want anybody else dictating its policy, even though there are aspects of the policy that could use a little constructive advice. For the present, policy coordination in a strict sense of the term is politically unrealistic. If Canada and the United States elect two people who choose divergent macroeconomic paths, all the agreements in the world will not force them to have the same macroeconomic policy. The United States will not adjust and neither will Canada.

The idea that Canada and the United States can coordinate better than the ten member states are coordinating in the European Community, which is not terribly well, is asking a lot. It is asking a great deal more to coordinate with Europe and with Japan and have one macroeconomic policy for the industrial world. It defies political reality.

That being so, two things need to be done. We have to let the free float work because that is an adjustment mechanism. Second, even with that, there will be regional or short-term inequities while the adjustment is working itself out. We may need some sort of institutional mechanism through which governments can ameliorate the consequences of diverging macroeconomic policies. These divergencies affect trading relationships. We can try to accommodate each other in particular problem areas until the adjustment is over and the divergencies are washed out of the system. In other words, we may need increased government contacts and some new institutional arrangement besides floating rates, because floating rates are likely to be unable to handle the political heat that governments will encounter.

Sectoral Agreement for
Trade in Computer Services

Traded Computer Services:
A Bilateral Beginning

ROWLAND C. FRAZEE

LAST FALL, in a letter to the prime minister of Canada, I proposed the initiation of talks with the United States aimed at bilateral agreement on traded computer services and at harmonizing the protection of privacy in both countries. To many observers those concerns might sound esoteric for a businessman. In fact since then, at meetings in both countries, one of the first questions asked is why the Royal Bank is interested in transborder data flows? Does the bank have a hidden agenda that explains raising a topic so apparently unrelated to its daily business—buying and selling money? There is no hidden agenda, but there is an answer.

Review of economic developments

From a trade perspective the economic history of the past fifty years might be characterized by three principal developments. The first, in the early 1930s as the world slid into the Great Depression, was a pervasive international tendency to erect barriers to trade in goods. As markets and prices collapsed, virtually every nation, including Canada and the United States, moved to put up walls to foreign competition, protecting and, so they hoped, strengthening domestic suppliers. The walls did not work; on the contrary, they deepened and prolonged the depression.

It took almost twenty years for the full folly of protectionism to become apparent. In 1947, international talks led to the second development, the creation of the General Agreement on Tariffs and Trade (GATT). One of its purposes then and now was to remove in an orderly, gradual, and mutually beneficial manner the tariff barriers erected during the depression. The results of removing barriers can be seen in the trade relationship between Canada and the United States. Our two countries share the largest bilateral trade in the world. On any working day Canadians and Americans buy and sell across our common border $600 million worth of goods and services. Annually, it is a $150 billion business. By 1987, over 90 percent of the goods that flow between the two countries will be free of duty or subject to duties of less than

77

5 percent. That achievement stands as a major monument to the value of international trade discussions and common sense.

A third major trade development of the past fifty years became apparent following World War II. That was the growing economic importance of trade in services as opposed to goods. And that trade has accelerated dramatically during the past ten years. Trade in services includes, of course, many very old and traditional industries, including my own, banking. It also includes insurance, transportation, broadcasting, and communications. It includes data transmitted from and to computers, and tourism, and consulting. The number of jobs, the value added, and the volume of international trade in those industries have grown at a phenomenal rate. While estimates are still imprecise, at least 50 percent of the economy in most developed nations consists of services. Furthermore, that sector is growing more rapidly than the economy generally or than world trade as a whole.

Thus the trade barriers of the 1930s were followed by the GATT negotiations to reduce them and finally by the increasing importance of trade in services. But with minor exceptions GATT does not apply to trade in services, and that is the problem. The area of trade that offers the best chance for both economic and social progress is also the area most in danger of protectionist interruption.

Problems of the information trade

The most exciting and most rapidly evolving section of services trade is based on what we might loosely call information technologies. The French coined the word "informatiques," or "informatics," meaning information that is stored, processed, and communicated by computers. While the capacities of these technologies are mind-boggling in their complexity, they are based on a simple concept. They *collapse* time and distance to the point that these words are essentially meaningless. Information, in the form of spoken words, written material, numbers, or pictures, circles the globe. It can be instantly available anywhere; and the costs of storing, processing, and moving it continue to drop at a dramatic rate.

These technologies offer us much more than fascinating gadgets. They provide a quantum improvement in the quality of life for vast numbers of ordinary people. Health care is better. The workplace is safer and less boring. Custom design and manufacture of consumer goods, from the housedress to the house itself, are easier, less expensive, and of improved quality. In education, in agriculture, in our environment, and our entertainment—in every aspect of our lives—we are living through a lengthy, often invisible, but profound revolution.

That revolution can be seen as bringing massive benefits to all mankind. But with those benefits come very real threats to national interests—commercial interests, political interests, social interests. As these technologies and their applications grow in importance and in usage, the perceived threats increase at exactly the same rate. I do not mean that American technology threatens Canadian interests. I mean that these technologies in general can act against specific national interests, and they can be used as policy weapons.

Let me cite just two examples. In the United States there is the Dresser case in which an American subsidiary company in France was prohibited from supplying equipment or technology for the Trans-Siberian gas pipeline project. What might we guess happened to the economic value and reputation of Dresser France the instant that access to expertise and information was removed? And in Canada in 1980 a new bank act required that selected bank data processing and electronic record storage be done within the country. What did that do to the operating costs of newly established foreign-owned banks?

The Dresser action was taken to support an American foreign policy position. And the Canadian action was taken not to support domestic data processing but to ensure unquestioned access and availability of data to Canada's inspector general of banks. Although the reasons for either action may have been misunderstood and the validity of the actions may be debatable, what is not in question is the sovereign right and ability of national authorities to interrupt flows of data and the very real costs, to someone, of such interruptions.

Without international agreements, those interruptions, those barriers to services trade, will increase, and we could well repeat the mistake with services that we made in the 1930s with goods. I do not believe that any national economy, and certainly not the international economy, can afford another mistake of that magnitude.

This is not a blinding or original insight. Policymakers in nations around the world have been discussing, analyzing, and trying to define these issues and their implications for nearly two decades. And there have been some significant successes—for example, the Canadian-U.S. satellite agreement. But in terms of multilateral agreement on broad principles for trade in services, relatively little has been accomplished, although this is more a tribute to the complexity of the issues and the sensitivity of national interests than it is to any failure of will, ingenuity, or energy.

Services trade and the private sector

The private sector has come very late to these concerns. With its traditional concentration on the next quarter, rather than the next quarter century, it has been applying these technologies, buying them, developing them, and using them as rapidly as they became commercially available. In the broad sense the private sector has not concerned itself with the long-term implications of the growth of trade in services and specifically the threat to our economies represented by potential restrictions on that trade.

It is time to do so. The proposals I made in 1983 were tangible evidence of a commitment to avoiding restrictions. In the case of the bank that I head, there are concrete reasons for involvement. The Royal Bank of Canada is the largest private-sector customer of telephone companies in Canada. We are also the computer industry's largest private-sector client. The Royal Bank's total expenditures on technology on a global basis in this fiscal year will be some $377 million. That figure includes the cost of hardware, software, telecommunications, and the people who operate them. Today it totals 20 percent of the bank's noninterest expenses. Twenty years ago the percentage was negligible; ten years ago it was still under 10 percent. The best internal estimate is that these costs as a percentage of noninterest expenses will climb by at least 1 percent annually for the balance of this century.

Anything we can do to get more bang for the buck from expenditures of that size is clearly going to be in our self-interest. We know that those expenditures are vital to the bank's ability to compete effectively in Canada and internationally, now and in the future. Information technologies in the broadest sense are the "how" of productivity increases.

That applies to us as a bank. But additionally, as bankers have known for centuries, we do best when our customers do best. Unrestricted flows of data and the availability of these technologies are important in terms of public policy, not just because they are useful to the Royal Bank of Canada. They are essential to the prosperous survival of business enterprise in its entirety—all business in Canada, all business in the United States, all business everywhere.

Because of the jargon and the technical complexity of the devices that provide information flows, some people may mistakenly think information flow is a technical issue. It is not, any more than war is purely a military issue or abortion simply a medical issue. This is a trade issue, an industrial development issue, and an international economic issue, and it requires the active involvement of businessmen from every sector. Information technologies and the hardware and software that are used to apply them offer productive and effective efficiencies to virtually every business enterprise. Freely available and sensibly applied, they will protect and create employment and prosperity, and it is vital we not allow them to be held hostage by protectionist instincts and reactions.

We have gone this long without international rules in part because the services and goods involved are somewhat new. They have run ahead of government regulations and in some cases they have made existing rules rather laughable. There is a true story, for instance, from a very successful data service bureau in Canada. The proprietor tells of an experience he had some years ago with Canadian Customs involving computer punch cards. Unused cards attracted a duty. But since the cards being imported were punched, the officer decided that they were used and that duty should be charged on them as waste paper, a few dollars per ton. Today, punch cards are declining in use, but in many ways the whole system of regulation is at odds with the realities of the new technologies. An international agreement that recognizes the new realities and ensures unimpeded flows will be to the general benefit of business enterprise in all industrial sectors.

Thus the Royal Bank of Canada is not involved in these issues purely as a selfless act of corporate good citizenship. It makes sound business sense for the bank and its customers to assist in resolving these issues. And because jobs, profits, and prosperity are in the self-interest of every government, resolving these issues is equally important to Ottawa and Washington.

An agreement on traded computer services

In 1983 I made a pragmatic proposal for moving toward agreement on regulating trade in services. First, instead of dealing in the multilateral context with over one hundred nations and an impossible complexity of conflicting and coincident interests, we might begin with negotiations between just two nations with a long and honorable history of cooperation, conciliation, and care for each other's mutual benefit. Second, we might limit discussions to a reasonable scope—not traded services as a whole, but the narrower area of traded computer services. What the two nations could agree to might possibly serve as a model for broader agreement later with other nations, and for a broader agreement on other service items and categories.

This proposal has generated significant interest and debate. The next steps, however, pose some difficulties, and I want to address three of them: achieving a definition, establishing a time frame, and encouraging an ongoing role for the private sector.

The term "traded computer services," while it rolls evenly off the tongue, is as difficult to define as the much more common phrase, "transborder data flows." But before two countries can talk, they need to decide exactly what they are talking about. The Canadian government is currently preparing a response to the first proposed definition received by them from the U.S. government.

I am not a technical expert and will not try to define which type of equipment or service should be included. The Canadian private sector will undoubtedly be consulted, and I will leave the issue of definition to others. But we should recognize that computer services and the associated hardware, telecommunications flows, and devices they involve all add up to a very wide-ranging and complicated list of items. Just as the area of services as a whole has consistently proved too wide for international negotiators to get their arms around, informatics may well be too broad to tackle all at once.

I am suggesting, therefore, that once an overall definition is reached the two governments seriously consider putting the goods and services in some kind of rank order for purposes of negotiations. They might start with just one or two discrete and easily described categories, adding more as basic principles are developed.

Intracorporate data flow, the movement of information between offices of the same company in different countries, is one such candidate. If data are to flow freely and unrestrictedly, there will have to be agreement on access—a clear understanding of the conditions under which a nation could interrupt such flows. Principles of privacy will have to be agreed upon, and participating countries might have to adjust related legislation. There would have to be safeguards and a mechanism for resolution of disputes.

Once such principles have been established in a very narrow area, then other types of services and goods could be discussed and measured against the same principles. The purpose of this approach, as with the original suggestion, is simply to provide a starting point and to avoid a time-consuming tangle in reaching a definition.

The second point has to do with the time frame. Both Canada and the United States face elections within the next ten months. While the processes of government are by no means in abeyance, the realities of politics mean that the attention of politicians may be more firmly focused on elections than on policy. Even without such diversions, this is a highly complex topic and it breaks new ground. Achieving agreement will take time, perhaps several years. That does not mean nothing can or should happen until 1985 or 1986. It may well be possible to develop partial agreement on individual services in a short time, and that small visible success would give both countries some sense of tangible progress. So, while politicians are renewing their employment contracts with the voters, there is an opportunity for government officials and private-sector advisers to accomplish substantial preliminary work.

And that brings me to the third point, the role of the private sector in these proposed government-to-government negotiations. Ambassador Brock, the U.S. trade representative, has already established consultative groups of private-sector corporations; my comments therefore should be understood to apply to Canada. Our minister with responsibility for international trade, the Honourable Gerald Regan, is fully committed to private-sector consultation and will soon be deciding on the exact mechanism. This Canadian advisory group or task force, in whatever form it takes, should have some particular priorities.

The essential purpose of this group is to advise government, in practical and credible terms, about what it finds acceptable and unacceptable in a possible trade agreement. That includes the following steps.

First, the task force should attempt to reconcile competing or conflicting domestic interests within Canada. Broadly, those might be characterized as the differing needs of the small supplier of information technologies and the large user. Both users and suppliers should participate in the advisory process. Newly established firms clearly tend to look across the street for business before they look across the border. They have a greater tendency to ask for special protection in their home market and to see less harm from reciprocal restrictions elsewhere. U.S. competition in all areas of information technologies is sophisticated, well financed, and supported by a large domestic market. While I think open competition between the two countries will ultimately be seen to be to everyone's benefit, it is inevitable that some small Canadian enterprises will view this development with initial trepidation. It would be useful if the private sector itself tried to resolve those differences rather than first seeking political adjudication by the government.

Whatever the structure of a Canadian advisory group, another essential element is at least informal representation from trade and industry groups as well as individual businesses. I think of the Canadian Advanced Technology Association, the Business Council on National Issues, the Canadian Association of Data and Professional Service Organizations, the Chamber of Commerce, the Canadian Manufacturers Association, and a number of others. Their expertise and background in the issues surrounding transborder data flows and their unique perspective on those issues would be of great value.

Next, I hope such a group can get rid of the phrase "free trade." It means different things to everyone and is an emotionally loaded concept both for those who expect to benefit and for those who fear they might lose. The goal is unimpeded flows of computer services, and if that is to be achieved, negotiated rules of the road, including safeguards for national interests, are required. The phrase "free trade" is a red herring, and it is counterproductive.

A Canadian task force should also bear in mind that these are not "Fortress North America" proposals. The sector is one that provides productivity benefits across the economy, and the talks should be a bilateral beginning to a multilateral solution. Both countries are committed to the GATT and other multilateral negotiations, and that will not change. Nor should it. But if bilateral talks can act as a catalyst or as a device to quicken the pace of parallel international discussions, they will be very useful indeed, and that is the spirit in which they were proposed.

A final consideration for a task force is the private sector's own behavior—and I refer specifically but not exclusively to large corporations operating internationally. What excites politicians and what will attract intervention, regulation, and trade barriers is corporate behavior that appears to take little account of national interests. Every government wants jobs for its citizens; moreover, it wants highly paid, technically advanced, economically creative and productive jobs. For example, world product mandates (under which subsidiaries of multinational companies specialize in production of particular products for the world market) have long been seen as a method by which multinational manufacturers can achieve the economies of scale and exporting success that help to harmonize the interests of the company with those of the countries in which it operates. World information mandates—a computerized global inventory system in one country, a global accounting system in another, and so on—might hold similar opportunities. Rigorous and uniform company codes of ethics in the handling of personal data and in other matters relating to privacy can also go a long way toward moderating the instincts of government to regulate. No government will abandon its concerns and leave the private sector to decide how and under what conditions business data will flow across borders. Clearly, however, by its own actions the private sector can make significant progress in reassuring nations that multinational flows of data and communications are not profoundly and permanently threatening.

It might therefore aid the process if the groups representing the Canadian and U.S. private sectors were to discuss the issues informally before reporting to their respective governments. Certainly within the private sector in each nation there is both the technical expertise and the understanding of business strategies that should develop solutions to accommodate each country's interests. Those interests are not necessarily identical; and while governments obviously bear the final responsibility for trade agreements, their work could only be assisted by such private-sector efforts. It might also be shortened.

Summary

Thus I see a major role for private-sector participation should the two governments decide to negotiate an agreement on traded computer services. While it may be considered as a separate sector along with the others on the bilateral agenda, that such agreement would provide substantial benefits to all industrial sectors deserves repeated and continuing emphasis. No company and no industry in either nation has a monopoly on the desire for productivity and competitive improvement. As Ambassador Smith, deputy U.S. trade representative, said of the overall sectoral discussions not long ago, these are joint efforts aimed at mutual goals. While every company in Canada and the United States could individually use the results of an agreement on traded computer services to the hoped-for benefit of its employees and shareholders, the overall rewards will be shared and international. As a stepping stone to multilateral progress in this area, such an agreement would be a historic and important example of U.S. and Canadian leadership.

In a paper published some time ago, Rodney Grey, Canada's former ambassador to the Multilateral Trade Negotiations, pointed out that the GATT was in the first instance based on principles developed in bilateral trade agreements between Canada and the

United States, as well as between the United States and Great Britain. Our two nations can lay claim to important roles in both the founding and the continued evolution of that immensely valuable mechanism. It is not, I believe, an overstatement to suggest that a clear opportunity to repeat that success is once again before us, and I would wish both governments well in their discussions.

Establishing Principles for Trade in Computer Services

HUGH P. DONAGHUE

THE PAST decade has witnessed a phenomenal growth in international services of all types. One of the major driving forces in this growth has been the merging of computer and telecommunications technologies, giving us the ability to transmit data economically between most cities in the world. Financial services, such as those represented by the Society for Worldwide Interbank Financial Telecommunications (SWIFT) network, have added new dimensions to international banking. Tourism, transportation, consulting, health, and educational services have crossed national borders in their offerings. But this growth has also raised controversy at international meetings over such issues as invasion of personal privacy and violation of national sovereignty. Thus we have a situation in which advances in technologies with enormous potential for enhancing economic welfare become matters of concern to the international community when the services provided by these technologies cross borders or, as we say, involve "transborder data flows."

Transborder data flows are generally defined as the electronic movement of data across national borders for storage and/or processing by a computer. These data flows therefore involve communications from a terminal to a computer in another country, from a computer to a computer in another country, or from a computer to an output terminal in another country. The concept is straightforward and sounds simple, but because one element exists in country A and the other in country B governments around the world have become uneasy. Their concerns involve protection and security of data, legitimate access to data by its owner, and differing national laws or, in many instances, no laws at all with regard to the treatment of data. As Rowland Frazee has noted in "Trade and Technology: It's Canada's Move,"* many of the issues are complex. Some involve suspicions by one party about the motives of another.

* Speech to the Canadian Club, Toronto, Canada, November 7, 1983.

87

*Transborder
flows of
personal data*

It is useful to trace the early development of governmental interest in and concern with transborder data flows. My initial introduction to it came in 1976 when questions were raised by the Swedish government about the practices of my company's data center in Sweden and the additional processing of data that was being performed in other centers in Europe. At issue was whether our procedures were in compliance with Sweden's Data Act of 1973.

In the early 1970s, Sweden had determined that abuses might occur in collecting and processing data on its citizens. In an attempt to prevent such abuses, the government established rules for the collection, storage, and dissemination of personal data on its citizens. It also wrote into law the right of a citizen to review information collected on him and, in some circumstances, to have it deleted or amended.

As the legislation was being drafted, Swedish authorities came to realize that a number of personal data files on Swedish citizens were stored abroad. This led to the question of whether the new legislation should address personal data that is stored only within the borders of Sweden or whether it should extend to data stored abroad. The government chose the latter course, and the legislation was applied to all data files on Swedish citizens regardless of where they were stored. This, in turn, led to the establishment of the Office of the Data Commissioner, where all files, domestic and international, would be registered. It was further required that any organization storing personal data outside the country would have to provide assurances that those files would receive the same protection they would if they had been stored within Sweden and that individuals would retain their review and appeal rights. Similar legislation was enacted in other European countries. The several laws differed in substance, however. The Council of Europe then called together a group of experts to try to harmonize privacy protection laws through a treaty.

The Organization for Economic Cooperation and Development (OECD), for its part, undertook a related exercise aimed at developing a set of voluntary guidelines. At the urging of the private sector, the U.S. government formed an industry advisory committee to protect the interests of the U.S. information industry. The first meeting of the Subcommittee on Transborder Data Flows of the State Department's Committee on International Investment, Technology, and Development was held on December 15, 1977. At that time the U.S. private sector was concerned that the various legislative acts in Europe to ensure privacy of data would be used to create nontariff barriers to flows of data across national boundaries. This concern was given substance by the statements of a number of prominent European officials involved in drafting such national laws. For example, at an OECD symposium on transborder data flows and protection of privacy held in Vienna in September 1977, Louis Joinet, at that time France's magistrate of justice, stated, "Information is power, and economic information is economic power. Information has an economic value and the ability to store and process certain types of data may well give one country political and technological advantage over other countries. This in turn may lead to a loss of national sovereignty through supranational data flows."

The first meeting of the drafting group on the OECD guidelines was held in Stockholm. The American delegation submitted a discussion paper that outlined its thoughts on a proposed set of guidelines. The drafting group used this paper and a European discussion paper to develop a set of OECD guidelines. Later, the U.S. delegation presented its paper to the Advisory Committee on Transborder Data Flows for consideration and comment. A new version incorporating comments and suggestions from both groups became the official U.S. position on the OECD guidelines. Successive meetings of the experts and drafting groups covered numerous substantive questions on personal privacy guidelines. Differences in approach to privacy protection were aired and compromise solutions considered. But although the delegates made considerable progress toward adopting draft guidelines, important issues remained unresolved—for example, whether manual files should be included, whether legal entities were to be covered, and whether special rules should be included to cover unusually sensitive data. By June 1980, however, the group of experts was able to agree on a final set of guidelines to which the Council of Ministers of the OECD gave its approval on September 23, 1980. Interestingly enough, the Council of Europe expert group had concluded its treaty draft just a week earlier. The principles laid down by the council's experts were essentially the same as those expressed in the OECD guidelines—which was not altogether surprising, since many of the European experts were members of both groups.

An OECD meeting was held on October 3–4, 1981, to review national progress on the guidelines. The United States was able to report that more than 150 major organizations, including a great percentage of those involved in the transfer of information across borders, had endorsed the OECD guidelines. While the privacy issue has not been put to rest, at least it has been put into proper perspective.

Government policies on computer technology

At the same time as they were developing national legislation to protect personal data, several European governments began inquiries into other aspects of the computerization of society, including the flow of nonpersonal data across national borders. European intellectuals led the way in asking about the possible economic, social, and political consequences of the advance of computing and telecommunications technologies. They foresaw threats to national well-being, employment, and sovereignty. A computerized society, it was suggested, would be vulnerable to manipulation by the owners and operators of the new technologies.

Once again, many in the United States were suspicious of European motives. Our initial reaction was that barriers would be raised to trade in information and telecommunications services and that European competitors would be given protection on the basis of spurious arguments about dangers to welfare and even to national independence. A report titled "Computerization and the Crisis of France," submitted to the French president in January 1978, did nothing to allay those fears. The authors noted that

> France must cope in a coherent, consistent way with dangers that imperil her economic balance, her social consensus, and her national independence. The soundness and sovereignty of any industrial nation depend on a balance of foreign trade, an adequate number of jobs, and the willingness of its citizens to abide by the rules of society. The correlation between the three objectives is longstanding. What is new is that today, spontaneous harmony among them no longer exists. Where, not so long ago, they were complementary, they have become antagonistic, if not mutually exclusive. All three demand attention at once, yet the isolated solution of any one of them necessitates action which jeopardizes the other two.*

The report went on to recommend that certain domestic industries be protected by the government. It suggested that government policy toward other data processing interests must be eclectic and pragmatic, taking into account the strengths and weaknesses of each. Service companies and small computer-peripheral firms ("peri-informatiques"), which are dynamic but splintered sectors, were to be supported. Research was to be

---

* Quoted in Alain J. Madec, "Private Investors Abroad," speech before the Southwestern Legal Foundation, October 1980.

granted the necessary funds. Incentives linked to action taken in industry were to be provided for the production of components. And, finally, once strategy had been defined, a fitting place was to be awarded to the French manufacturers of large computers.

These recommendations were accepted by the French government, and a commission was established under the chairmanship of Alain J. Madec. His report to the government of France has now been completed. At a meeting at the OECD held in October 1980, Madec revealed some of the thinking of his commission with regard to issues raised by transborder data flows. He told the OECD conference that

> International exchanges of information concern an asset of universal value which can generate wealth or power to those who hold it. Oddly enough though, these flows are largely untouched by the traditional rules governing trade in products: they seldom appear in the accounts of those concerned and, where made between related bodies, are rarely invoiced at their "transfer price." Neither are they recorded by the customs, and their very volume often remains unknown to the authorities.
>
> Consequently, the free circulation of data implies far more than the concept of free trade, providing opportunities, without any possibility of control, for fraud, espionage, dumping and profit flight. Owing to lack of adequate means of measurement, moreover, the impact of information flows remains distinctly underestimated.
>
> It is therefore necessary that states succeed in jointly promoting better understanding and control of information flows, in order to preserve the advantages of free circulation and ensure that its effects are more equitable. This cooperative effort has become an urgent necessity. If economic analysis fails to keep in step with growing awareness of real or supposed dangers, protectionist barriers will be bound to arise, especially in the Third World, and would then take decades to dismantle, as the history of the General Agreement on Tariffs and Trade shows.*

Madec's observations coincide with those of others in the field. Cooperative efforts are under way in the OECD and other organizations to gain a better understanding of the implications of transborder data flows so that the free flow of data may be preserved.

Canada has also been regarded with some suspicion in the U.S. data and telecommunication service industries. That is why many welcomed the Frazee initiative and are eager to enter into discussions with their Canadian counterparts. I firmly believe a con-

* Ibid.

structive discussion can lead to a better understanding of the concerns of both sides and possibly to an agreement on a basic set of principles that will enhance prospects for economic growth in both countries.

Restrictive government policies

Before I turn to thoughts on a set of principles, let me touch briefly on three examples of governmental actions that send the wrong signals. Two of these involve Canada and one the United States. All are complex and involve issues beyond transborder data flows.

The first has been mentioned by Rowland Frazee in his comments on the Bank Act of 1980. The actions of the Canadian government with regard to access and availability of data to their bank regulators are surely legitimate. The Bank Act would not have raised the kind of questions it did, however, had it not been preceded by a report of a Canadian government economist somewhat earlier. That report noted the amounts and types of data flowing from Canada to the United States for processing and storage and then estimated the number of jobs that could be created in Canada if all of the processing were performed within the country. The estimates ran from several thousand in 1978 to some 23,000 by 1985. This in turn led to the expression, "the export of data is equivalent to the export of jobs." Many people in the United States viewed the Bank Act as a first step toward a requirement that data processing be performed in Canada if in any way feasible.

The second example involves an activity called "remote diagnostics" in which many U.S. computer manufacturers engage. At the National Computer Conference in Chicago on May 6, 1981, Michael Blumenthal, chairman of Burroughs Corporation, raised the subject in an address titled "Transborder Data Flow and the New Protectionism." He stated,

> Privacy restrictions are already affecting our Remote Support Centers. These are regional computer systems designed to monitor and diagnose problems with customers' computers, guiding on-site repair work. This work can involve the transfer of sensitive data from a customer's system to Burroughs computers, especially if the customer is a government agency. Recently the Canadian government denied a petition by Burroughs to dial into the government computing system to service their hardware. Canada cited privacy as the reason for the denial. We will have to see whether local control becomes the issue in non-security situations, and what occurs when our diagnostic system happens to be located across a national boundary.

A third instance of intervention involves the United States. The U.S. government cited foreign policy and national security issues when it decided in 1981 to withdraw its support for the International Institute for Applied Systems Analysis (IIASA), the only East-West think tank. The IIASA was established in the early 1970s, during the heady days of détente, as a means of bringing together intellectuals from East and West to conduct in-depth studies on such issues as world energy, agriculture, and informatics. In support of its decision the U.S. government cited dangers from the potential access of Soviet scientists resident at IIASA to commercially available data bases such as Lockheed's Dialog. European response to this action was one of indignation. One English publication argued that much of the technical information the United States was reluctant to supply to the USSR had its origin in Western Europe, not in the United States. The article went on to say,

> We hold no brief for the Russians, the East Germans and the rest of that crew, but we do believe that countries considering large-scale dependence on U.S. supply sources should know the U.S. attitude toward freedom of information and whether that freedom be a conditional one or a genuine one. We also regret that the U.S. industry spends a lot of time huffing and puffing against real or imagined "nontariff barriers" whilst closing its eyes against barriers erected by its own government against non-U.S. customers with the will and the means to buy publicly available information—whether assembled in the U.S. or elsewhere—on a normal commercial basis.*

These are but three of numerous examples to demonstrate how complex the issues can be. Perceptions on the part of one party about the motives of another play an increasingly significant role, and often a misleading one, in the former's reaction. The problem is made more difficult because there are no agreed-upon principles that would provide guidance to both parties.

Toward a tele-communications policy

The United States still lacks a comprehensive set of objectives for a policy on international telecommunications and information that has been agreed upon by all parties involved—users, service providers, and equipment suppliers, as well as the various agencies of the government. There is some progress, however. Two advisory committees established by the State Department are considering these issues. The U.S. Preparatory Committee to the International Telecommunications Union (ITU) deals with issues

---

* Quoted in Madec, "Private Investors Abroad."

under study by that organization. The Subcommittee on Transborder Data Flows of the Advisory Committee on International
Investment, Technology and Development considers issues under
study by the OECD.

Recently, at the request of the government, a task force was
set up composed of private-sector members from the U.S. Business
and Industry Advisory Committee to the OECD and the U.S.
Preparatory Committee of the ITU. This task force includes
experts from the user business community, service providers,
international record carriers, and equipment manufacturers. It is
attempting to establish the first comprehensive set of U.S. objectives for international telecommunications and information policy.
It will also attempt to develop strategies, define exposures, and
compile a list of official international and regional forums where
these objectives might be pursued. The task force will forward
its completed proposals to the respective advisory committees for
submission to the various government agencies and departments
involved.

At this time the task force has developed and circulated a set
of guiding principles to form the basis of the more detailed
objectives. A current draft of these principles states:

> In order to promote the growth and efficiency of the telecommu-
> nications and information industries, as well as the telecommunication-
> dependent industries, the following principles should apply:
>
> —Open international marketing of information processing and
> telecommunications equipment should be encouraged on a fair and
> competitive basis without restrictive trade barriers.
>
> —Users should have freedom to choose from competitive suppliers,
> including telecommunications agencies, for the supply, installation,
> and maintenance of their customer premises equipment.
>
> —There should be an unrestricted and competitive international
> market for value-added (enhanced) telecommunications and infor-
> mation services.
>
> —The encouragement of innovation in and development and
> application of new products and services should be through compet-
> itive market forces.
>
> —Recognizing that there will always be a requirement for an
> efficient public telecommunications network, it is essential to continue
> to encourage the development of high-quality services in both de-
> veloped and developing countries.
>
> —To provide maximum interconnectability among national tele-
> communication networks and services, reasonable basic standards
> should be established on an international basis with users' and suppliers'
> participation.

—Users should have the freedom to choose from available basic transmission services; included among such services should be "transparent" services, such as full-period leased circuits, which provide users with the greatest flexibility and ease of use.

—Prices charged for regulated telecommunication services should normally be based on the cost of providing the services.

—While attention should be paid to the protection of individual privacy, proprietary information and national security, the general and traditional free flow of information among nations should be preserved in the interests of the advancement of the world economy.

These principles were developed from a U.S. perspective and as such may be too narrow to satisfy those desiring an agreed-upon international set of principles. They are not all inclusive and are still subject to discussion and debate in the United States. They provide a basis, however, for a dialogue between private-sector groups in the United States and Canada. I believe Rowland Frazee has such a discussion in mind. The objective would be to arrive at a statement of the objectives the two countries would like to achieve in the field of international data and telecommunications services and information technology. These objectives could then serve as a basis for negotiation by the two governments. In turn, an agreement by the United States and Canada could be a model for negotiating an international standard.

General Discussion

Roy Matthews of the Economic Council of Canada wondered whether the new items on the trade agenda—trade in services and high technology, for example—are necessarily different in kind from more familiar items. As a case in point he mentioned Donaghue's comments about national laws or rules ostensibly designed to protect privacy but which may be used as a nontariff barrier in the field of data flows. He asked whether these rules were very different in principle from health or safety standards established for good and sufficient national policy reasons but which then may be used as a means of protection. Specifically, would it not be possible to approach issues of this kind functionally as nontariff barriers of a readily comprehensible kind? Otherwise, are we not likely to confuse and befuddle the issues, making workable definitions and acceptable solutions more difficult to achieve?

Donaghue generally agreed, adding that in many areas in which nontariff barriers have been identified, GATT rules provide some guidance. But in the case of data flows, things are not well defined at all. While discussion continues about whether standards set by other countries will become true nontariff barriers, the industry and the volume of trade are growing at a very rapid rate.

Donaghue noted that there is an opportunity before actual barriers have been raised to try to resolve problems, real or imagined. Discussions with the Europeans on the problems of protecting privacy very early showed that a significant social issue needed to be addressed. That issue has been put on a much firmer basis today because of the OECD exercise. That is why 150 organizations in the United States, mostly very large companies, have endorsed the OECD guidelines and have developed policies and procedures conforming to them. On the other hand, those on the data commissions and others in Europe have learned that multinational firms in general are good corporate citizens, that there has been very little misuse of the data in their possession, and that where questionable cases have occurred they were clearly mistakes rather than the result of deliberate actions.

MacLaury called on Robert Mathieson of AT&T, an expert in this field and a member of the U.S. Chamber of Commerce's Committee on Canada-U.S. Relations, to comment.

Mathieson began by noting three realities. The first, he thought, is that there seems to be a broad commitment in Canada to the goal of greater economic integration with the United States and certainly to reducing transborder frictions, but not at the sacrifice of cultural and political sovereignty. The second reality is that it will take a number of years to reach any major part of that goal. The third and perhaps most important point is that this is a political year on both sides of the border and that political interests are likely to prevail over other considerations.

Turning specifically to the high-technology sector and the related trade and transborder problems, Mathieson said that there were differences between it and the more traditional sectors. For example, the Royal Bank's initiative on access to computer services is very sharply focused. It is far less clear which industrial sectors or parts of sectors are really on the table for serious negotiation. There is obvious uncertainty about what the mandate is or what kinds of trade-offs or deals can be made.

A second difference is that the Royal Bank's initiative addresses a rapidly growing, high-technology sector with world competitors on both sides of the border. In the traditional sectors there are mature industries in which anyone would be a fool to bet that a year from now employment would not be lower than today. The risk in negotiating free trade in these traditional sectors is that people will look back and say that their government leaders did them a disservice when they cut a deal in 1984. If so, progress toward more lasting economic integration could be compromised.

Another difference, Mathieson noted, is that Frazee stressed an eventual multilateral approach, which means that GATT problems cannot be treated cosmetically. The issue is already on the table in the OECD working party, and the International Chambers of Commerce on both sides are involved. Because it is already in the multilateral arena, Canada and the United States are pretty much bound to make sure that it remains there.

Furthermore, the private sectors are taking the lead in studying and analyzing the subject. In traditional trade negotiations, government has taken the lead; and while it may go through the usual mechanisms of private-sector consultations, the leadership role is clearly with the official side.

Finally, the Royal Bank's initiative may lead to a statement of agreed principles governing data flows. Experience and interpretation would then allow an evolution toward a kind of formal code. By contrast, industrial-sector agreements, if any, must be wrapped up pretty tightly from the first, which may take some doing. Mathieson thought that it would be prudent to keep the Frazee initiative apart from but parallel to the industrial-sector discussions so that any disappointments occurring to the latter do not carry over to the former.

Robert MacIntosh of the Canadian Bankers Association said that he did not wish to defend the Canadian Bank Act but that he could expand on a point that Frazee had made because this legislation did establish a precedent for restraints on transborder data flows.

Frazee had noted that one purpose of the act was to provide for sovereign access to stored data. Obviously, a regulatory body cannot perform its duties unless it can have access to the records relevant to those duties. But when this piece of legislation was drafted, the purpose of achieving or ensuring sovereign access was obscured by a protectionist purpose. The concerns expressed by Donaghue had some validity because in fact there were software producers in Canada, small ones, that had made representations to the government and to the drafters of the act, charging that one of the large banks had access to a particular piece of software in New York City through which it was massaging some data. The purpose was protectionist, and the language of the legislation does go beyond the notion of access. It says, "A bank shall maintain in Canada a record showing for each customer particulars of the transaction between the bank and that customer . . . and shall maintain and process in Canada any information or data relating to the preparation and maintenance of such records."

The first question is, what does the word "access" mean? After all, data can be stored anywhere in the world—in Timbuktu if you will. There is no problem about having a host computer, as the North American System does, in San Mateo, California, to keep records for Visa cards all over the world. It is not necessary to process or store data in Canada to access the data there. Despite the Bank Act, large Canadian banks, for example, have New York offices where they record foreign exchange transactions daily through computers and perhaps forward the data to the head office. Small subsidiaries of American banks in Toronto or Montreal daily supply information to their head offices in New York.

So in fact the transfer of corporate information of that sort has not apparently been impeded thus far. The act might be used for that purpose, however, and undoubtedly Canadian software companies would like to do just that. Thus there is a danger that the sovereign access provision as written could be used to prevent intracompany transactions.

Privacy, on the other hand, is a question of unauthorized access and not really a transborder data issue at all. It is an issue of a general character. Unauthorized access is unauthorized access, at home or abroad. Whether a nonresident, a party from outside the country, could access files is not separable from the issue of whether fellow nationals can access files.

MacIntosh added that he believed telecommunications protocols and international standards, especially for data transmission, are being used as protectionist devices, especially by some European nations that see in them means of preventing U.S. technology from taking over the computer market in Europe. In this connection, governments will have to pay more attention to the operations of the International Standards Organization (ISO). About 250 ISO committees deal with international standards, including data processing standards, banking standards, and so forth. These standards can be and are being used, especially by members of the European Community, to freeze out North American technology by defining standards that make procurement impossible. The Canadian and American members who sit on ISO committees, both for the private sector and for governments, should be paying more attention to whether the standards being developed are compatible with North American technological and industrial policy objectives.

Frazee responded that the software companies had indeed made representations to the Canadian government in connection with the Bank Act because they were trying to protect their interests, at least to some extent. Their principal representations were to ensure that the big banks did not go beyond the provision of computerized services directly relating to banking. That was the possibility that really bothered the Royal Bank. It was a very effective lobby.

The consideration mentioned by MacIntosh may well have been in the minds of the legislators. But Frazee observed that there is absolutely no question about the position of the inspector general. His concern is only with access to data.

If the data are stored in another country, that country could take a unilateral action to prevent access. Canada has had some experiences, for instance, with certain banks involved with customers in tax havens such as the Bahamas and the Cayman Islands. Although these cases did not exactly involve the electronic transfer of data, they did have to do with data in one jurisdiction concerning the nationals of another.

MacLaury returned to the question of privacy. MacIntosh had treated the issue as almost entirely one of unauthorized access, but it seemed to MacLaury that there was another aspect. In the case of Sweden that had been mentioned earlier, the issue was how much information on its citizens could a country permit to be stored, whether in folders or electronic files, in a different jurisdiction with different laws. Access might be authorized for information on individuals that would not be available in their home country under home country law. Thus, unauthorized access may cover much of the issue of privacy, but it may not cover it all.

Edward Fried of the Brookings Institution asked whether the United States and Canada, in responding to Frazee's initiative, could not under what seem to be fairly ideal conditions work out something that would be consistent with GATT and that might provide considerable impetus, if the two countries were successful, in breaking through the very complicated international discussions that Donaghue described. Specifically, why couldn't the two countries get on rather quickly with the modest first steps of the agenda that Frazee outlined in his paper?

Donaghue replied that, in the first place, Canadian business interests are not unanimously in favor of this idea. A Toronto *Globe and Mail* article, "Industry Warned Free Data Flow Threatens Jobs," of February 10, 1984, noted, "The data processing industry is dead set against Canada getting involved in any agreement with the United States guaranteeing the free flow of data between the two countries. At present, data flows without barriers between the two countries, but principally from Canada to the United States." The opposition is there, principally from small companies and, from their point of view, for very legitimate reasons.

In the second place, Donaghue noted, the United States may have problems with ensuring privacy. Unlike European privacy legislation, which is very broad in coverage, U.S. legislation has been confined to narrow areas and is very thorough where it applies. First of all, it applies primarily to the public sector—the Fair Credit Reporting Act, for instance. But it does not apply to the private sector or to industry in general. This is why, in promoting the OECD guidelines, the United States tried to show that its companies do indeed protect the privacy of personal data. Nonetheless, it would be very difficult to get legislation through the Congress, especially with an administration that has a deregulatory point of view. Before the Carter administration's term expired, it had several proposals for extending privacy legislation to other areas, but these died in the new administration.

Mathieson said that being less experienced he was perhaps more optimistic. The U.S. and Canadian Chambers of Commerce, in consultation with people such as Hugh Donaghue and those from the trade associations, are preparing a statement of private-sector principles that would acknowledge the relatively free regime that now exists in data flows between the two countries. It would also encourage the respective governments to keep the flows unimpeded and to oppose any steps toward establishing barriers.

Formalizing data flow guidelines may require something less than congressional action, although there should be some assurance of congressional support. In updating the Satellite Communications Act of 1972 about a year and a half ago, commitments were made through an exchange of letters between the Canadian secretary of state for external affairs and the U.S. secretary of state that codify governmental positions with respect to providing alternative technological support and assuring freedom of choice for the customers of satellite communications facilities.

Donaghue also noted that many developing countries feel an empathy with Canada's continued interest in nation building and in cultural sovereignty. Years ago the railroad was the instrument for nation building; today it is the computer and the information industry. But Canada is not the only available model. Brazil, for instance, has a highly protectionist attitude toward transborder data flows. So if Canada and the United States can agree on a treaty or something halfway to a treaty, it would send an important message to the rest of the world.

Frazee commented that he was not familiar with the article from the *Globe and Mail* but he thought the emphasis of the headline did not reflect general attitudes in the country. He said that an apparent principal shareholder of a software company in Canada has been highly vocal in opposing suggestions for a bilateral agreement, but a number of organizations have given either unqualified or qualified support to it. The Royal Bank, Frazee noted, has received only two or three negative letters.

Frazee also pointed out that computer service companies in the United States tend to be large, well developed, market oriented, highly capitalized, and highly competitive. In Canada, with some exceptions, they tend to be small, undercapitalized, and perhaps in need of some government preference or protection in order to survive. But if Canadian companies ever want to get ahead, they must look to broader fields and broader markets. One of the principal areas of conflict is between the big user in Canada and the small provider of these services. In establishing guidelines, some consideration would have to be given to these small companies. They ought to have a reasonable period of time to enable them to become competitive in North America and perhaps throughout the world.

Frazee also emphasized that a bilateral agreement should not be an end in itself. While Canada has more to gain from a bilateral pact, the United States has more to gain from a multilateral agreement. A bilateral beginning could, however, set a pattern for multilateral agreements.

He urged Canadians to recognize that they have some important businesses, which, if they are to remain competitive, need technology. Not all the technology will be produced in Canada; the country is not big enough or advanced enough. Canada does, however, have some very successful high-technology companies such as Northern Telecom. Its steel industry is probably more competitive and more highly developed than that in the United States. But Canadian companies need technology, and Canadians should be prepared to emulate the success the Japanese have had in importing technology. That technology will increasingly involve computers. If there are disruptions to the flow of computer-based data, then Canadian industry generally will suffer. The goal is not to protect the software industry in Canada but to protect all Canadian business, which has to be competitive.

Philip Trezise of the Brookings Institution asked how a bilateral agreement between the United States and Canada in this field would put pressure on the Europeans and the Japanese to enter into a multilateral agreement. What is there about a bilateral agreement that would create pressure points for Tokyo and Brussels?

Frazee said that he would not use the word "pressure" but rather would think of a bilateral agreement as an example to the rest of the world. GATT had such a beginning when Cordell Hull instituted discussions with Canada and Great Britain on mutual trading arrangements.

The Europeans—and perhaps the Japanese as well—are very apprehensive about the lead that the United States has in the broad range of services. It may be losing ground in goods, but it is gaining ground almost daily in services and is balancing its payments to a considerable extent through earnings from services. If an agreement could be reached between Canada and the United States that did not obviously appear to be a disadvantage to the smaller country—and there is no way either would wish to permit that—it could serve as an example that the United States could use to reassure those countries that are expressing great reluctance to enter into any kind of discussions in the broad range of services.

Energy Issues:
Trade and Investment

Hard-Earned Lessons about U.S.-Canadian Energy Relations

JAMES R. SCHLESINGER

IN DISCUSSING the future of U.S.-Canadian energy relations it seems appropriate at the outset to recall the words of one of the wisest of American philosophers, Samuel Goldwyn, who once commented, prediction is difficult, especially about the future. I take his admonition to heart. Though Marshall Crowe and I negotiated the treaty for the Alaska highway pipeline some seven years ago, and though Mitchell Sharp and I labored to implement that agreement, all of us are still waiting for something to happen. So predicting the future does remain rather difficult.

Energy trade and politics

We all recognize the advantages of trade. They are clear, logical, and always there. By contrast, the world of politics is based not on logic but on emotion, perceptions, and historical experience. It is a quite different world. Nevertheless, energy policy can never be abstracted from the world of politics. For example, despite the clear-cut benefits of trade, Canada imposed restraints on the export of hydrocarbons during the L970s. Those restraints were especially burdensome because they disrupted the complex transportation systems that move these fuels and because certain U.S. refineries are dependent on imports of Canadian crude oil. Nevertheless, it does underscore how readily the actual as well as the presumed benefits of trade may be abandoned.

That period of self-imposed limits on exports is now behind us—at least temporarily.

At a more general level, the advantages of trade are frequently not accepted with respect to natural resources. These are perhaps the best example of wasting assets. They are "irreplaceable." Thus, a concern inevitably persists in the minds of nationalists regarding the distribution of returns from those assets. To sacrifice irreplaceable resources for a handful of dollars must always seem suspect. Partly for this reason, the benefits from energy trade are likely to remain incompletely realized.

When Mitchell Sharp commented that "you must understand our peculiarities," he really meant that we Americans should appreciate Canada's special virtues. And when he said, "We wish to remain different," he meant it. There is in Canada the same ambivalence about proximity to the United States as that revealed by Porfiro Diaz, former president of Mexico, when he observed, "Poor Mexico, so far from God, so close to the United States."

Sharp's wise comments reflect the perspective of someone from the political world. Those of us who come out of the world of economics—or of Chambers of Commerce—do not always appreciate or even understand the world of politics. Politics remains the art of the possible. It does not seek to impose the logic of free trade on resisting electorates. Thus with respect to the prospects for wholly unfettered trade, we are unlikely to see what George Ball earlier described as "a rearguard action against the inevitable." The Canadian desire to be less in the shadow of its great neighbor will long be with us. It will never altogether disappear, and it will always make ambiguous the pattern of trade relations in energy, however appropriate the triumph of wholly free trade might seem on economic grounds.

As a result of depressed economic conditions, we are currently in a period in which economic logic and the appreciation of the benefits of trade come to the fore. Nationalist sentiment on either side of the border is at a low point—to put it precisely, a postrecession low. As Sam Johnson might once have said, "Nothing collects a man's mind so much as the notion that he—corporately or nationally—might go belly-up." That sobering sense of peril has been notable in this recession and postrecession period that has helped to produce an apparent oil glut. Nationalism may be something of a superior good, as the economists define it. As incomes rise and the fear of possible impoverishment recedes, nationalism is likely, once again, to rear its head.

Economic and political aspirations tend to move in opposite directions. Consequently, there is a cycle with respect to nationalism. For those Americans who have been critical of Canadian nationalism in recent years, I merely point out that the Atomic Energy Commission had at one time banned imports of Canadian uranium, allegedly on grounds of national security but actually because representatives from the Western states had successfully harassed the commission at a time of diminished demand for uranium.

Moreover, in 1971 the Canadians were not given any relief from the 15 percent import surcharge imposed by President Nixon. Yet, ironically, not so long before that the United States had begun to promote the concept of a continental energy policy. The combination of the surcharge decision and the pressure for a continental energy policy led to the deepest freeze in U.S.-Canadian relations that anyone can recall.

The continental energy policy was a clear example of what George Ball described as "a common plan to exploit North American energy resources." Such expressions mean, in the eyes of nationalists, that the wasteful Americans would be making off with Canada's irreplaceable resources. (Our southern neighbor, Mexico, has been and will remain even more sensitive than Canada regarding the national patrimony.) Throughout this period, Canada's ambassadors in Washington rightly warned that it was impolitic to talk about a continental energy policy and that it would be far more constructive to talk about energy cooperation on a pragmatic basis. Such admonitions were valid not only with respect to the immediate problem in that period of high sensitivity, but in the longer run as well.

Grandiose concepts for continental energy development may be eagerly embraced in Midland, Texas, or in Calgary, but they do not provide a solid political basis for longer-term policy. In the long run, we would be well advised to handle bilateral energy relationships on the basis of pragmatism rather than on the basis of a free-trade ideology. Treating energy exchanges on a pure free-trade basis may not be a live option. Since energy raw materials are wasting assets in limited supply, times of trouble will inevitably bring emotionalism to the fore. In energy matters the United States itself moves from complacency to panic and back again. Panic will bring impulsive or irrational reactions. That cycle is scarcely confined to the American side of the border. It should probably be taken for granted that whenever energy problems reappear, we shall see the return of such emotions.

Nationalism is unlikely permanently to disappear. Thus, given the past history and the future prospects, pragmatism should be the key. Let me now turn to some specific energy issues in U.S.-Canada relations.

Natural gas Natural gas necessarily will be the primary traded fuel because the North American continent will continue to have a deficit in oil. Nonetheless, in recent years Canadian gas sales have plunged dramatically—far below the authorized level. Why? The reason is quite simple: prices are too high. As the U.S. market has weakened, contracts with Canadian suppliers have been subjected to *force majeur*.

In formulating its policy for gas exports, Canada must carefully examine the market and the characteristics of the regulatory regime in the United States. Until 1978 that regime had been established by the Phillips decision of 1954, which resulted in the imposition of rigid price controls on interstate gas but no constraints on the price of intrastate gas. For the Canadian gas exporter, that was truly the golden age. In the past it was believed that the American consumer had been the principal beneficiary of the Phillips decision, but that was a dubious proposition. Ironically, it was the Canadian exporter who became a principal, if not the principal, beneficiary of the Phillips regime.

The dual market created by the American regulatory system did an immense (if anomalous) favor for Canadian producers: it discriminated against American producers and eventually regulated many of them out of the market. Ultimately price controls led to severe shortages in the interstate market. Canada was the supplier nearest at hand. The result was that Canadian producers found ideal conditions in which they could move gas into a market that subsidized their sales. They could sell gas at higher prices, there being a steadily diminishing competition from domestic producers, particularly in markets near Canada.

Normally in competitive markets, it is the high-cost supplier who is the marginal supplier. The Phillips decision overturned these standard conditions. Not only did rigid price controls keep much of domestic production out of the interstate market, but in addition, Canadian sales in the American market were subsidized by being rolled in with lower-priced domestic supplies. Even though they were the high-cost suppliers, Canadians were not, in practice, the marginal suppliers.

But any golden age must come to an end. The point of recalling the Phillips regime is to contrast that situation with what exists today. Passage of the Natural Gas Policy Act in 1978 has resulted in de facto decontrol of all save old gas supplies. It is increasingly becoming necessary for Canada to adjust its policies in light of present regulatory conditions rather than the conditions of the past.

Under this newly competitive regime, the key word has become "net-back." The price of gas at the point it is burned must compete with alternative fuels, now most notably residual fuel oil. At the wellhead, the price can be no higher than the residual or net-back after transportation and distribution costs have been deducted. Sales will fall for any supplier, including those sales undertaken by the Canadian government, if he fails to compete at the burner tip. In recent years, as the implicit subsidies for Canadian gas have declined and as more domestic suppliers have moved into the interstate market, Canadian sales have eroded dramatically.

No longer is the normal rule of competitive markets being reversed. The high-cost producer, the Canadian producer, has indeed become the marginal supplier. Sales may well continue to decline unless Canadian policy is changed so that Canadian gas effectively competes with other fuels at the burner tip.

In short, the gyrations that we have seen in Canadian gas sales over recent years are no anomaly. They were to be expected as the special advantages of Canadian gas in the American market disappeared and as Canada failed to make the necessary adjustments. The formula that Canada has employed to set the export price of its gas is now wholly obsolete. It is uncompetitive and it presupposes an American regulatory system that has now disappeared. In recent months Canadian policy has begun to adjust— belatedly and insufficiently. The export price for gas has been reduced from $4.94 to $4.40 per thousand cubic feet. Nonetheless, that decline is insufficient to recapture Canada's share of the U.S. industrial market.

I have sometimes felt that the cross-border trade in natural gas can only be understood through a theory of comparative lunacy reflecting the ebb and flow of policies on both sides of the border. In her domestic market Canada has realistically concluded that it can only move increasing volumes of gas by pricing at 70 percent of the price of oil. Yet, simultaneously, it seems to believe that the American market will bear a substantially higher price. Such inconsistent premises provide a parallel to the earlier creation in the United States of a dual market, which was similarly assumed to be immune to the normal market forces. Like the United States, Canada will have to rid its policies of illusions and inconsistencies if it is to take full advantage over the long run of the proximity of the large American market.

Recently, the United States has, through Department of Energy Secretary Hodel, announced changes in its import policy. The new policy applies, however, only to new contracts, which makes it largely irrelevant to Canadian sales under ongoing contracts. Nonetheless, the announcement does provide an opportunity for Canada to reconsider its export strategy. Because changes are unavoidable, what would be better than to seize the occasion and to blame the Americans for any change in policy?

American demand for gas is now picking up. By about 1986, a snug supply in the United States is expected, if not a shortage akin to those of 1977 and earlier. Canada's gas sales can therefore expand again. Whether they do will depend on whether Canada makes the adjustments that permit it to meet the competition. The magnitude of those adjustments will, of course, depend upon how unfolding developments in the Persian Gulf affect oil supplies and oil markets.

Before I close my remarks on gas, I want to mention the Alaskan natural gas pipeline. There has been a great deal of indignation in Canada because the Americans failed to deliver on the construction of that pipeline. Moreover, it is frequently said that Canada would never have proceeded with the pipeline arrangements if it did not have an ironclad guarantee from the United States that construction would proceed.

Let me say quite simply: there is a difference between image and reality. At this time, Canada should not want to have the Alaskan pipeline completed and in operation, simply because it would further diminish Canada's prospective gas sales to the United States.

Other issues   In a sense, the issues surrounding the export of electric power are structurally similar to gas. Canada has been reluctant to enter into long-term contracts for the export of electric power, especially baseload power. The provinces have been as ambivalent as Ottawa, reflecting the same attitudes as those toward gas—an instinctive resistance to foreign exploitation of the national patrimony. That attitude is, however, now rapidly changing—as economic realities have come to overshadow economic nationalism. But, as in the case of gas, prices must be competitive. A high-cost supplier must inevitably wind up being the marginal supplier. If Canada wants to provide baseload power for the United States, it must price below the cost of alternative American capacity. Today those costs are very high, especially in the northern United States, and thus provide an enticing prospect for Canada.

Regulatory problems, regulatory risks, the threat of acid rain, and ascending costs of nuclear plants give Canada the chance to earn substantial foreign exchange through the sale of electric power. Canadian facilities can be built now, at least in part, to serve the American market. As the demand for electric power rises in Canada, sales to the United States can decline. Happily, the flow of water is not a wasting asset.

As for oil, North America will never again be a surplus area. The present Canadian surplus appears transitory and is likely to disappear. In the United States, demand for oil will gradually rise and production will slip, so that by the early 1990s the United States is likely again to be importing 8 million to 8.5 million barrels of oil a day, as it did in 1977. Canadian oil exports can scarcely solve that problem. Moreover, when the world moves back, as it eventually will, to a condition of tight oil supplies, a recrudescence of Canadian nationalism seems likely if not inevitable.

I should like to offer a conclusion. And I want to cite, as an analogy, a contention of real estate experts. They frequently say that the three most important determinants in real estate sales are location, location, and location. For harmonious Canadian-U.S. relations in energy matters, the three most critical elements continuously to stress are pragmatism, pragmatism, and pragmatism.

Within the industrial world energy exports will always be characterized by some degree of ambivalence. We would all be ill advised to forget the simple reality that nationalism will not and probably should not disappear in Canada. Consequently the notion that trade in energy raw materials can become wholly unfettered and based solely on comparative advantage remains an illusion that we should avoid. In part, we need to avoid the illusion of unfettered free trade to avoid unsound investment decisions, but avoiding that illusion is even more important in order to preserve reasonably harmonious relations between Canada and the United States in this touchy area.

An Assessment of the Recent Record in Canada

MARSHALL A. CROWE

I WOULD LIKE to begin with a brief comment on nationalism, which loomed large in James Schlesinger's remarks. Raising prices when supplies become tight should not be identified with nationalism. Rather, it is straightforward market-related pricing, as is a reduction in prices now when the market is slack.

By the same token, the criticisms I will make about Canadian energy policies should not detract from my credentials as a Canadian nationalist. Nor do they suggest that Canadian policy should be designed to meet U.S. interests, although in fact I believe they can be in the interest of both countries. Instead, my view is that in some respects Canadian energy policies have been ill designed to serve Canadian needs.

Canada's energy position

A few facts will help to set the stage. Canada is still a very important oil producer. Last year, according to the *Oil and Gas Journal*, Canada ranked eighth among the oil-producing countries of the world, with an average daily output of just under 1.5 million barrels a day. In 1983, Canada was also the second largest source of crude oil and products imported by the United States. In the late 1960s and early 1970s, Canada was by a considerable margin the largest source of U.S. oil imports, although it had to fight a pretty steady battle to maintain access in the face of the U.S. import restrictions. Canadian exports of crude oil and petroleum products to the United States in 1983 averaged about 486,000 barrels a day out of total U.S. imports of a little above 4 million, or about 12 percent. We continue to import into eastern Canada some 300,000 barrels a day, so that in 1983, Canada became a net exporter of oil for the first time in a decade, that is, since the disruption that began with the Arab embargo of 1973. Net exports of petroleum and products were valued at $2.1 billion.

This modest achievement, seven years ahead of the 1990 oil self-sufficiency goal of the National Energy Program (NEP), has been attained in spite of, not because of, that program, the impact of which on exploration and development in western Canada, where all the oil and gas still come from, has been almost entirely harmful. Some backing off of the NEP with respect to pricing and taxation over the course of 1983 has been essential to whatever improvement in performance has been achieved.

The progress made in relation to oil still leaves Canada well below its peak, when production exceeded 2 million barrels a day and we were selling more than 1 million barrels a day to the United States. However it could be the beginning of a healthy recovery to a level at which Canadian oil production could again provide both the bulk of Canadian requirements and some significant export income. It is noteworthy that much of the oil being exported is heavy oil and that, in spite of the costs of enhanced recovery techniques and the need to dilute it for pipeline transportation, the prices currently available in the U.S. market make it economical. Established reserves of heavy oil are adequate to at least maintain current output levels for many decades. Facilities to upgrade heavy oil, put on a back burner by NEP taxes and prices, now seem imminent once more, and they could add substantially to our supplies of light and medium feedstock for Canadian refineries or for export.

Beyond heavy oil are the huge reserves of oil sands. An Alberta Energy Resources Conservation Board report forecasts an increase in oil sands output from the present level of about 160,000 barrels a day to some 875,000 barrels a day by the end of the century. Oil sands plants were another casualty of the NEP. The new taxes, uncertainty as to whether world prices would be allowed, and the long delay during the gestation of the new program and the price negotiations with Alberta ended all new megaprojects. However, in the last year, with price assurance and relief from the federal petroleum and gas revenue tax (a kind of federal royalty), a number of smaller projects have started.

Ideally the oil industry in Canada will continue to develop with a secure domestic market operating on the basis of world prices and access to the U.S. market. So long as the United States needs to import 4 million or 5 million barrels a day of crude oil and products, it should be manifestly in our mutual interests for the United States to take whatever of this is available from Canada. We may have our curious ways that even our best friends find annoying, but we have never deliberately disrupted a committed flow of oil or gas to U.S. markets.

Turning to natural gas, our trade relations also have a considerable history and are even more significant than oil to both countries. In 1983, Canada provided about 80 percent of U.S. gas imports and between 4 percent and 5 percent of total U.S. natural gas demand. Still, our gas export record was the poorest for many years. The volume exported, 713 billion cubic feet, was well under 50 percent of the total of existing licenses, and perhaps only about a third of the amount Canada was prepared to export if all the licenses approved by the National Energy Board had also been approved in Washington. Nevertheless, gas sales still netted some $4 billion of export revenue.

Regulatory failures and remedies

Canadian-U.S. trade in natural gas has always been heavily regulated. With the benefit of hindsight I would say that much of that regulation, and I speak only about the Canadian side, has been misguided. The National Energy Board Act requires that gas for export be found by the board to be surplus to reasonably foreseeable Canadian needs, taking into account trends in the rate of discovery. (The same rule has always applied to electricity and was made applicable to oil in 1973.) In regard to natural gas the board has essentially enforced this statutory restraint by requiring that established reserves equal to twenty-five years of current Canadian consumption be on hand over and above the sum of any proposed new exports and the total of remaining approved exports at the time when new exports are being authorized. Once such a calculation has been made, the board has never retroactively changed it to reduce an approved export, even though in the mid-1970s reserves reassessments seemed to point in that direction.

During a critical period, beginning four or five years ago, when the U.S. market was still eager for more gas, the board complicated its formula with a series of academic and bureaucratic deliverability hurdles that virtually ensured no additional gas would be available for export. Thus when new contracts might have been signed, our regulatory regime could not find a surplus, although all the evidence from the industry indicated that there were huge volumes of shut-in gas that required only firm markets to be connected and brought on stream. Fortunately this self-defeating approach was dropped. In its export report of January 1983, the board found an immense surplus, 17.5 trillion cubic feet, or about one year's total U.S. consumption at today's reduced level, available for new exports over and above 40 trillion cubic feet set aside to meet future Canadian needs and 12 trillion cubic feet already, at that time, licensed for future export.

The board proceeded to allocate 11.5 trillion cubic feet of this surplus to new export licenses, but by the time this was accomplished the U.S. market was no longer there. As a consequence, very little of this new export gas has received the parallel approval required in Washington.

As the board was gradually bringing itself around to approving much larger exports, the government was regularly, if not deliberately, reducing the available U.S. market by constantly raising the gas export price. Pricing had formerly been the responsibility of the board, which had indeed increased the export price from the very low levels still prevalent in 1973. They were increased from Canadian $0.30 per thousand cubic feet initially to Canadian $1.00 in 1974 and by stages to U.S. $2.30 by 1979. These prices were well within what the market would bear. They were reasonably related to marginal energy costs in both countries, and they were made gradually, with time for adjustments. After the Iranian oil crisis in 1979, gas export prices were tied more directly to oil prices, effective control was taken away from the NEB, and the price was rapidly escalated to a high of U.S. $4.94 by April 1981, a price that resulted in a major loss of markets.

Since that time the price has gone down again to a base price of U.S. $4.40 per thousand cubic feet with an incentive price of U.S. $3.40 per thousand cubic feet for amounts over a base volume, generally 50 percent of contract amounts, and there is every indication of further moves to try to restore this trade to a market-based competitive pricing regime. It is widely expected that the response to the gas import guidelines recently announced by Secretary Hodel will be some form of return to negotiated pricing between buyers and sellers, within certain limits and requiring some form of governmental approval but without the inflexible government price setting of recent years. If this does not happen, the gas will not be sold.

Now that the government has decided that Canada does indeed have a large exportable surplus of natural gas and is almost agreed that the gas cannot be sold if the price is not competitive, it may be possible for this trade to recover to its former level and then to resume growth. Although pricing has been erratic, there has never been any deliberate Canadian interference with the flow of gas under existing licenses. Even involuntary shortfalls because of purely physical production problems have been very rare, and the present surplus of shut-in gas in Canada is such that curtailments of any sort are highly unlikely.

What is needed now is a period of some commercial stability with a minimum of government direction on either side of the border to allow private negotiation of contracts that meet whatever broad guidelines are found necessary. On the U.S. side this means that contracts must be commercially viable and flexible enough to be adapted to changing market conditions. On the Canadian side the surplus for future Canadian needs has already been thoroughly provided and will not be a barrier for many years. There will also no doubt be some Canadian price criteria, but current studies in Canada show that in many U.S. markets a price competitive with U.S. gas or other fuels, after deducting all transportation costs, could still yield a better net-back at the Alberta border than is currently received for internal Canadian sales.

Greater utilization of the pipeline systems involved will of course reduce the unit costs and improve the economics. The problem of underutilization of the transportation system is particularly relevant to the high costs of transmission over the prebuilt southern parts of the Alaskan Natural Gas Transportation System, which is now moving only some 40 percent of the Canadian gas originally contracted for. To the extent that Canadian gas is priced out of the U.S. market, economies of scale from greater utilization of the pipeline will not be realizable.

While oil and gas are much the most important, they are not of course the only items in our energy trade. Sales of electricity annually exceed $1 billion, and there is potential for growth to three or four times the current level. If all energy sources are aggregated, Canada in 1983 provided about 16.5 percent of all U.S. energy imports. Canada's net energy exports last year, virtually all to the United States, produced net earnings of $7.3 billion: petroleum and products, $2.1 billion; natural gas, $3.9 billion; and electricity $1.3 billion.

To conclude on a broader perspective, I would argue that producers and consumers of energy in both countries would benefit from a moratorium on grandiose energy policies and programs. Governments are perhaps not notably worse, but certainly no better, than private companies when it comes to forecasting. It is much harder for governments to disengage from their mistakes, however, and their mistakes do a lot more harm because they can coerce whole industries to follow their lead.

Consequences of investment regulation

Before the advent of the National Energy Program, the petroleum industry in western Canada was an important source of strength for the economy, providing incomes and jobs to a wide range of manufacturing and service activities in eastern Canada. Of each dollar spent for machinery and equipment by the petroleum industry of Alberta, an estimated $0.55 is spent in Ontario and Quebec; and for every job created in the producing province by oil and gas activity, two more are created elsewhere in Canada. At the very least the NEP brought recession to the Canadian petroleum industry a couple of years earlier and made it more severe than would otherwise have been the case. It added an immense bureaucratic overlay to doing business in this industry. The decisions of companies as to where to explore were heavily influenced by new incentives to move to the offshore and northern frontiers. These incentives were financed by massive new taxes on the old producing areas of the West, which already were depressed by price controls. In the name of Canadianization, which had been progressing quite nicely already, a number of carefully designed discriminations against foreign companies were built into the new regulatory regime.

Concurrently with the implementation of the NEP, the Foreign Investment Review Agency (FIRA) began to take a much tougher line on any transaction in the oil and gas industry. Although government spokesmen continued to reiterate that they were not opposed to foreign investment, their actions were a better guide to their intentions. Replacing a tax-based depletion system with a program of government grants in aid of exploration, scaled in accordance with the degree of Canadian ownership, allowed discrimination against companies controlled and owned by non-Canadians without risk of violating international tax agreements. The expropriation of 25 percent of all interests in the Canadian lands, that is, the North and the offshore areas, was not discriminatory. It took from Canadians and non-Canadians alike. Nevertheless it had a heavier impact on non-Canadian companies because under the new regime the Canadians would at least have access to the higher levels of exploratory grants. Its most severe impact came from its application to discoveries made before the NEP was introduced, for example, the Hibernia oil find.

During this period, FIRA not only prevented new foreign investment in the oil and gas industry but rigorously applied its mandate to block and delay and extract concessions even when it was dealing only with a transfer from one non-Canadian owner to another. This kind of case comes up frequently as an incidental consequence of mergers and acquisitions involving companies outside of Canada when an acquired company has interests in Canada that cannot be transferred without FIRA approval. During the past year or so, FIRA's attitude on many kinds of transactions has moderated, but it is not yet clear that there has been any change regarding the petroleum industry. In short the deliberate discouragement of foreign investment was an integral part of the whole NEP package.

Some of the consequences of this energy investment policy were perhaps not quite what was expected. A number of Canadian companies thought the time was right for foreign acquisitions. There were stories in the United States that Canadian government policies were in effect devaluing foreign oil and gas assets in Canada to make them easy pickings for Canadian buyers. In fact many Canadian acquisitions of foreign holdings were made at the very top of the market. Those who were bought out got excellent deals by any standard and, in many cases, the Canadian acquiring companies, confronted soon afterwards with spiraling interest rates and the oil and gas glut, still face a long lean period of trying to work their way back to financial stability. By ruling out any significant access to foreign equity capital, FIRA restrictions added to their problems, making it much more difficult to shift part of their heavy bank indebtedness to equity financing.

Petro-Canada, along with the shareholders of the companies it bought, was the main beneficiary of this whole process, and it had the immense advantage of not having to raise its own money. In his latest report the auditor general of Canada stated that he has not been able to obtain any information from Petro-Canada about the real costs to the Canadian taxpayer of its acquisitions. The Canadian Ownership Account set up by the NEP produces close to $1 billion a year, obtained from a special tax of about $1.15 per barrel on oil and about $0.15 per thousand cubic feet on gas. According to the auditor general, Petro-Canada did not even have to raise the interest costs of interim bank financing for its $1.7 billion purchase of Petrofina Canada Ltd. The interest was paid out of the Canadian Ownership Account but, by some very innovative bookkeeping, Petro-Canada was still able to use it as a business expense and so reduce its tax liability by some $60 million.

In the preelection atmosphere in Canada, a scramble is under way to disclaim and disown this whole national energy program. The Conservative opposition party has of course been quite forthright about it, but a number of the Liberal leadership hopefuls are now also suggesting that they do not know quite where it came from but that certainly they were not the parents. In the field of energy, governments have a terrible compulsion to try to take charge, especially when things are going well. To adopt an injunction once given by Canadian economist Harry Johnson to our Central Bank, the energy motto for governments for the next few years at least should be "Don't just do something, stand there!"

General Discussion

ROBERT DUNN commented that Canada's refusal to sell gas because the price was too low could be based not on nationalism but on the expectation that prices in the future will increase faster than the rate of interest and that leaving gas in the ground was therefore preferable to selling it at low prices. Electricity produced from hydro power, however, is different. It is possible to store only a limited amount of water behind a dam. Once the reservoir is full, power that is not used is lost.

Schlesinger said that the Canadian government's policy, adopted in 1979, was based on the wrong formula. It was not based on a projection that future gas prices would increase faster than the rate of interest, but on an argument that the price of gas should be equal to the price of crude oil in terms of BTU equivalent. That formula is wrong. Besides, gas sold to Canadian consumers is priced by the rule of thumb that it should cost no more than 70 percent of the price of crude oil in BTU terms. That formula is about right.

Crowe doubted that setting gas export prices had much to do with any theoretical notions about the relationship with oil prices. The object was to get the most possible from export sales. If a ratio to oil prices did not provide the number that was wanted, some other formula would have been found. In fact, a half dozen different criteria for pricing gas exports were used during that period.

As a matter of fact, in a period of crisis when there were perceptions of a shortage, it made some sense for Canada, as a net importer of oil, to argue that it should get the same price for hydrocarbons it exported as it had to pay for hydrocarbons it imported. However this is not a principle that can be imposed on customers when the situation changes.

Crowe said his objection was that price increases continued beyond the time they were feasible. He had supported increases in gas prices from $0.30 per thousand cubic feet to $2.40 per thousand cubic feet because he believed the market would support such increases. He opposed raising the price to $4.90 when the gas could not be sold at that price.

Schlesinger said he also saw nothing wrong with raising prices to meet a market. Nor did he consider such action to be nationalistic. To him evidence of nationalism consisted in withholding supply, which Canada did in 1980 in the case of oil. Each year Canada told the United States that its sales of oil to the northern tier refineries would soon have to end. That action he regarded as nationalism.

Crowe replied that Canada had to reduce exports to the United States because of restrictions on imports to its own east coast. It had to look after Canadian needs. Within that limitation it exported as much oil as it could move.

Schlesinger demurred, pointing to Canada's cutoff of light oil to the United States while it encouraged the flow of heavy oil. He emphasized, however, that the United States was hardly in a position to criticize Canadian nationalism on this point. Three U.S. administrations have gone to the Congress to obtain authority to export Alaskan oil to Japan. Each has been refused on strictly nationalistic grounds.

Rashish said that notwithstanding nationalistic policies, the consensus was that Canada could not eventually avoid the exigencies of the marketplace. Schlesinger had argued, further, that nationalism would again become a factor should supplies tighten.

He then asked whether it would be possible for the United States to provide some market assurances to Canada through a long-term energy agreement. Canada might then use such an agreement during an emergency to counter nationalistic pressures to preserve the energy patrimony. Or might trade-offs in other areas serve the same purpose?

Schlesinger agreed that longer-term commitments might provide governments with protection against the irrational policies that they are going to be under pressure to adopt in periods of stringency. For that reason governments need to plan ahead during periods in which they are not under political pressure, so as to have a structure in place to resist these irrational tendencies. Rashish's suggestion is one example of such a broad strategy.

Julius Katz of Donaldson, Lufkin, & Jenrette said that Rashish's comment about a broader agreement indicated the need to clarify earlier references to the continental energy discussions that took place in the 1970s. Discussions on a continental energy policy were not an American plot to raid Canadian energy resources. In fact, the term "continental energy policy" originated with the

Canadians. Those discussions began in an effort to find some way to deal with Canadian complaints about American pressure on Canada to reduce its exports of oil to the United States. There were also other problems, including restrictions on imports of uranium from Canada and a desire to find a rationale for a general energy policy. The problem of security of supply was a central issue in the discussion, including the concern that if there were another embargo on oil, the need to supply eastern Canada would lead the Canadians to curtail their exports to the United States.

A Concluding Perspective

Managing Canadian–U.S. Interdependence

ALLAN E. GOTLIEB

IF THE FUTURE of the Canadian-U.S. relationship is one of increasing economic interdependence it will also be a future of increasing complexity from the standpoint of the two governments. It would be irresponsible to embark on an era of increased economic interdependence without monitoring the effects of the process. The process includes not just the negotiation of sectoral free trade arrangements or further liberalized trade but also expanded investment flows and the continentwide provision of services. Monitoring these effects may lead to occasions when one government or the other will want to intervene or regulate or change the pattern of things. This will cause disagreements between the two federal governments, among the states and provinces, and with our respective private sectors. Are we well equipped to handle these problems? Do we need new mechanisms to deal with them? These are the questions that I would like to address.

Extending linkages

In determining whether we can manage the challenges of the future, we should recognize that if the degree of economic interdependence between Canada and the United States is already unprecedented, the future will confirm and extend the existing links. To take one example, major investment decisions that might previously have been made on the basis of a national market are in many sectors already being made on the basis of a continental market. This has been particularly true in the automotive sector but is also the case in many of the emerging high-technology sectors.

This tendency is likely to increase. It means that the trade and industrial policies of the two governments will likely have an even greater impact on where new investments are located. An illustration of the extent to which the continental marketplace is already the reality is that the growth in Canadian exports to the United States in 1983 equaled twice the absolute value of our exports to Japan, our second largest national trading partner.

In the service sector the degree of interdependence will soon match what already exists in the manufacturing sector. The introduction earlier this year of international toll-free telephone dialing, permitting, if the subscriber pays for it, transborder access to "800" numbers for the first time, is of no small significance because it means that many services can now be offered without regard to the locations of supplier and customer.

One of the best examples of a problem generated by increased economic interdependence is extraterritoriality. The assertion of jurisdiction beyond national frontiers on the basis of ownership of property or the economic consequences of an action is directly linked to the growth of trade, investment, and financial flows. This area has the greatest potential for giving rise to serious disputes. Indeed, U.S. policies toward the exercise of extraterritorial jurisdiction are the greatest gift the United States makes to economic nationalism in Canada. If U.S. multinationals, which own or control close to half of Canadian manufacturing, are subject to the foreign policy and national security interests of the United States, the potential for difficult conflicts will exist. The challenge is to take advantage of the benefits of economic interdependence without suffering the consequences of conflicts of jurisdiction.

Canadian self-confidence in the viability of our institutions and our capacity for self-generated economic development has increased significantly over the last ten to fifteen years, in part as a result of efforts to strengthen our national cultural industries, our basic energy sector, and our entrepreneurial abilities. Irrespective of the merits of one specific sectoral policy or another, Canada is now a more self-confident society, and this greater self-confidence permits a more detached assessment of sectoral free trade than would have been possible some years ago.

Notwithstanding this progress in strengthening Canadian institutions, economic and cultural instruments, and nationhood, I believe self-interest dictates that Canadians will continue to have three serious preoccupations as we approach a future of increasing economic interdependence. Are we getting a fair deal? Are we maintaining a satisfactory degree of political and cultural identity? Will we be able to sustain an acceptable level of economic independence? It is against this background that I would like to examine the adequacy of our methods of managing the relationship.

Problems and
reconciliation
procedures

Until now we have submitted relatively few issues to arbitration. Two notable exceptions in recent years are the GATT panel review of elements of undertakings made by foreign investors under the Canadian Foreign Investment Review Act (FIRA) and the submission to the International Court of Justice of the Gulf of Maine boundary dispute. This approach to settling disputes has been somewhat limited over the years for two reasons: to be effective, both sides must agree to implement the arbitral decision, and there must be a previously agreed set of guidelines or rules that adequately cover the issues embraced by the dispute. There is, however, an increasing recognition that if impartial analysis of a problem is presented carefully, it does not have to be seen as a matter of winners and losers and can be a useful way of taking contentious issues out of the political theater. I think this recognition is in part a reaction to the way in which the FIRA panel worked. Whether the enthusiasm for external mechanisms will be as great once the Gulf of Maine decision is known remains to be seen.

There is, however, a category of issues that might benefit from third-party or independent analysis. One could include in this category issues that arise because we adopt different approaches to achieving common objectives. Some extraterritoriality problems might fall into this category. For example, both Canada and the United States share the common objective of ensuring that the international financial system is not used to evade taxes or to launder funds obtained in fraudulent or criminal activities. Although the United States considers that it has the right to exercise judicial power to obtain evidence located abroad regardless of the laws of foreign countries, if it does not have to exercise such jurisdiction in order to obtain the evidence, the conflict need not arise in practical situations. To convince the United States of the efficacy of other procedures may well require establishing a joint committee of lawyers and bankers from several countries to devise guidelines and procedures. At least some of the work may be better done outside formal governmental structures. Indeed, some very useful work is being done now by legal counsel to banks in both our countries.

In many cases, however, there are neither previously agreed rules nor common objectives with conflicting tactics. There are simply different policies of greater or lesser fundamental importance. This is the category of problems that is most likely to expand if, as I expect, the degree of economic interdependence between Canada and the United States continues to grow.

One example is the regulation of services. Until recently, we did not recognize the importance of ensuring that regulatory regimes covering such activities as transportation, communications, and professional services need to mesh smoothly and efficiently. However, as the providers of these services move into each other's markets, it becomes increasingly clear that there are natural and regulatory advantages that will allow one country to get a larger share of the business than the other. The reasons for this are often complex. They may have little to do with the internal efficiency of the service provided and more to do with the political geography of the continent.

Unlike the issue of tariffs for goods, the regulation of services within a country does not lend itself readily to tariff-cutting formulas or multilateral trade-offs. It would be very difficult, if not impossible, to devise a formula whereby three countries might liberalize their respective regulatory regimes for three different types of services to different extents and to measure in advance the likely economic consequences of this. Even if such a formula were possible, the degree of opposition from the various private sectors would be much greater than exists in trade negotiations. Each sector is distinct, and if trade-offs occur between sectors, the adjustment process will be difficult. Mobility of capital and labor between, for example, civil aviation and trucking is obviously limited. Because of the difficulty of launching a multilateral negotiation embracing certain of the service sectors, we may be moving into a period in which we go beyond multilateralism. The traditional balancing in trade negotiations of gains in one sector against losses in another may have to be replaced in some (but not all) service sectors by the negotiation of balanced deals in narrow sectors.

If one is not careful, a specific sectoral approach may not in some cases yield sufficient scope for trade-offs, with the result that very little progress would be made. This kind of issue cannot be resolved through third-party arbitration, and it may be that the liberalization of regulations in the service sector may require a much greater level of political involvement and domestic consensus building than has beeen necessary in traditional trade negotiations. To facilitate such a process, it might prove useful to commission an independent analysis of a sector and an examination of the pros and cons of various levels of continentwide restructuring. There will be an even greater need for our respective private sectors to develop closer working relationships.

The above example focuses on the question of getting a fair deal. It lies at the core of disputes relating to trucking, civil aviation, and to a lesser extent, certain more traditional types of trade, including the auto pact and a range of products that are the subject of investigations under section 201 of the Trade Act.

Another category of disputes associated with the growth of economic integration relates to the perceived need in Canada to limit U.S. involvement in certain sectors for broad cultural policy objectives or in order to preserve and enhance the national identity. It is extremely difficult to solve such disputes because the United States usually sees them in trade or economic terms while Canada usually sees them in fundamentally noneconomic terms. The most obvious examples of this are in the area of communications policy. They arise because for many Canadians the preservation and enrichment of our distinct cultural identity is not possible without some protection of the relevant domestic market and the provision of incentives to local production. Resolving issues of this nature will require a recognition by the United States of the legitimacy of the basic Canadian objective and an examination of how this objective can be achieved in a manner that minimizes the adverse economic impact on the United States.

Then there is the question of "linking." I agree with the conventional wisdom in Canadian-U.S. relations that we should not link issues. There are two very important reasons for this. Many issues involve important principles: to trade off, for example, missile testing in Canada for progress on acid rain in the United States would be repugnant to most thinking citizens of both countries. In addition, given the relative sizes of the two countries, if a bilateral balancing approach were taken, the United States would always stand to lose less in relative terms than Canada would if the issues were not resolved. This is not a good position from which to bargain. On the U.S. side, given the plethora of individual interest groups that stand to be affected by changes in the Canadian-U.S. relationship, linkages are avoided because of the problems involved in trading off one of these interest groups in favor of another. Congress has departed from this principle occasionally, but I think it is one of the good working rules of the game, even if, as a result, progress on individual disputes is sometimes very slow and causes impatience and frustration among politicians on both sides of the border.

Improving the process

I believe that I have dwelt adequately with the problems associated with dispute settlement in an era of increasing economic interdependence. It is now time to make some positive comments about how to prevent these problems from getting the better of us.

First, because the Canadian-U.S. relationship is a diffuse one, none of us should be upset if we fail to keep all aspects on track all the time. It is simply beyond the power of federal governments in our two countries to control all the elements of the relationship. It is also contrary to both our views as to the appropriate limits to the legitimate exercise of power by government. In the United States the division of powers between state and federal governments is further complicated by the separation of powers among the three branches of government at both levels. This does not mean that we should give up when practices at the state or provincial level affect the other country adversely or when judicial interpretation of congressionally mandated actions contravene stated government policy. But it does argue for some sympathy if the speed of response is a bit slower than usual.

Canada will continue to press the U.S. administration on unitary tax and to object to an approach to private antitrust damage suits that allows the recapture of treble foreign damages, even though we know that state governments lie behind the unitary tax problem and that Congress is the real stumbling block to progress on treble damages. We will continue to press, but we know that it will be difficult for the United States to meet our concerns fully at once.

Although the relationship is diffuse, it is not particularly fragile. It can stand a constant menu of irritants without getting indigestion as long as it is possible to make even modest progress on most of the items.

The second point is that some issues can be defused by further study. It might be possible in a sector such as civil aviation to improve the atmosphere by having an independent consultant analyze the likely effects of various degrees of liberalization on the industries and consumers of both countries. In addition, periodic meetings of technical experts together with policy officials can provide a framework for mapping out solutions. In trucking, the establishment of a consultative mechanism has meant that potentially disruptive licensing decisions can be examined calmly and without precipitate retaliatory action. Another encouraging sign is the existence of informal consultative arrangements between the two sides on communications matters. It is still too early to tell how useful these bodies will be or whether they will continue to meet for long, but they have the special merit of bringing all the key players together from public, private, federal, and state sources in two very pluralistic societies. That is a good beginning at getting to a broader understanding and analysis of conflicting regulatory approaches. The same is also true in energy, where the energy consultative mechanism has been reactivated after being dormant for a couple of years.

Third, there will have to be some compromises associated with further economic interdependence. Some changes will be hard to accept. In the field of financial services, for example, the degree to which we penetrate each other's market will be much greater than in the past. This could make it more difficult for Canada to conduct its own monetary policy. Is this desirable? To what extent is it consistent with the Canadian goal of maintaining a separate political and cultural identity? These are broad political questions, and their resolution will probably require informed political debate and compromise.

Fourth, there are some disputes that will require high-profile Canadian lobbying efforts in the United States. There is no natural domestic political constituency for Canada in the United States. This is not a normative statement; it is simply a fact.

With closer integration, Canada will become more and more influenced by the sideswipe effect of developments in the United States. Because we are a foreign country, we neither can be nor do we wish to be too closely a part of the domestic political process. Our primary points of entry into the U.S. political system must be and should be the State Department and the rest of the executive branch. But just as the relationship is diffuse, so the players in the United States are diverse. It is essential for us to bring our message to the principal actors on a particular issue, wherever they may be, and to form alliances with appropriate domestic constituencies. I make no apology for advising members of Congress on Canada's views about the extraterritorial reach of the Export Administration Act or for letting the Supreme Court know how Canada views the legal issues involved in requiring an international corporation to follow a course of action that violates the law of another country.

To return to my two questions: Do we have the mechanisms with which to deal with the increasing economic interdependence that the next few years are likely to bring, and are there improvements that we can make?

We may be able to make somewhat greater use of intermediation and third-party review than we have in the past. There may also be a need for a greater degree of political involvement in what appear to be technical issues, because some of the issues will have a lasting and fundamental impact on Canada at least.

But there is no magic formula for solving bilateral issues: they are one of the costs of increasing economic interdependence and we need not get too excited about the phenomenon of public disagreement. Indeed the more we progress in the direction of sectoral free trade and liberalization of the service sector, the more likely it is that we will generate problems that are not susceptible to easy solutions. This is not a reason to stop the pursuit of trade liberalization; it is a reason to be imaginative and innovative in looking for ways to reconcile interests.

Finally, I question the view, at least from the Canadian perspective, that Canadian-U.S. relations are still managed in an ad hoc way. Canadian policies toward the United States are now by and large centrally managed, comprehensive, and strategic within the limitations—positive limitations in my view—posed by the federal system and by the essential fact that the great bulk of what goes on between the countries is in the hands of the private sector. This is illustrated to some extent by the Shultz-MacEachen meetings four times a year. We are able to deliver, and in viewing our relationship strategically we are saying that we can mobilize ourselves in support of essential objectives.

Conference Participants

Matthew J. Abrams
President, Canamco

Raymond J. Ahearn
Specialist in International Trade and Finance, Congressional Research Service

C. Michael Aho
Office of Senator Bill Bradley

Mark A. Anderson
Department of Economic Research, AFL-CIO

Willis C. Armstrong
Member, Senior Review Panel, Central Intelligence Agency

Ellen Reisman Babby
Executive Officer, Association for Canadian Studies in the United States

George W. Ball
Former Under Secretary of State, United States

William E. Barreda
Director, Office of International Trade, U.S. Department of the Treasury

Shelly P. Battram
Vice-Chairman of Committee on Canadian Law, American Bar Association

Thomas K. Brewer
Director, Office of North America, U.S. Department of Commerce

William E. Brock
U.S. Trade Representative

Kenneth J. Brown
President, Graphic Communications International Union

Calman J. Cohen
Vice-President, Emergency Committee for American Trade

William T. Coleman, Jr.
Senior Partner, O'Melveny & Myers (Trustee, The Brookings Institution)

Terry R. Colli
Staff Economist, Canadian Embassy

Roy T. Cottier
Senior Vice President, Corporate Relations, Northern Telecom Limited

Marshall A. Crowe
Former Chairman of the National Energy Board, Canada

135

William R. Cuming
Executive Assistant, International Operations, The Timken Company

John M. Curtis
Director, International Economics Program, The Institute for Research on Public Policy, Ottawa

Thomas D'Aquino
President, Business Council on National Issues

Rimmer De Vries
Senior Vice-President, Morgan Guaranty Trust Company

Wendy Dobson
Executive Director, C. D. Howe Institute

Hugh P. Donaghue
Vice-President, Government Programs and International Trade Relations, Control Data Corporation

Charles F. Doran
Professor of International Relations and Director of Center of Canadian Studies, The Johns Hopkins University

Diane Lady Dougan
Coordinator for International Communications and Information Policy, U.S. Department of State

Robert M. Dunn, Jr.
Professor of Economics, The George Washington University

Maurice C. Ernst
National Intelligence Officer for Economics, Central Intelligence Agency

Jill Feltheimer
Legislative Assistant, Office of Congresswoman Olympia Snowe

Eric M. Forman
Acting Director, Office of International Emergency Measures, U.S. Department of Energy

Henry H. Fowler
Former Secretary of the Treasury, United States

Rolland G. Frakes
Senior Vice-President, Marketing, Novacor Chemicals Ltd.

Isaiah Frank
Professor of International Economics, School of Advanced International Studies, The Johns Hopkins University

Rowland C. Frazee
Chairman and Chief Executive Officer, The Royal Bank of Canada

Kenneth Freed
Bureau Chief, Canada Bureau, Los Angeles Times

Edward R. Fried
Senior Fellow, The Brookings Institution

Earl H. Fry
Special Assistant, Office of the U.S. Trade Representative

Kiyohiko Fukushima
Manager, Washington Office, Nomura Research Institute

Ruth S. Gold
Special Assistant to the Assistant Secretary for Economic and Business Affairs, U.S. Department of State

Patrick Gossage
Minister-Counsellor, Public Affairs, Canadian Embassy

Allan E. Gotlieb
Ambassador of Canada to the United States

Joseph A. Greenwald
Counsel, Weil, Gotshal & Manges

John A. Hannah
President Emeritus, Michigan State University

Kathyrn Hauser
Office of the U.S. Trade Representative

Gary N. Horlick
Partner, O'Melveny & Myers

Gary Hufbauer
Senior Fellow, Institute for International Economics

Barbara Jacob
Counselor for Trade and Economic Affairs, Delegation of the Commission of the European Communities

Gorden Jansen
Research Associate, The Conference Board of Canada

Robert W. Jerome
Capital Strategy Research, Inc.

Philip S. Jessup
Vice-President, William H. Donner Foundation, Inc.

Julius L. Katz
Donaldson, Lufkin, & Jenrette Futures, Inc.

Samuel I. Katz
Professor, Georgetown University

K. D. Keegan
Vice-President and Treasurer, Texaco Canada Ltd.

Jeremy Kinsman
Minister, Political Affairs, Canadian Embassy

A. E. Klauser
Senior Vice-President, Mitsui & Co. (U.S.A.)

Shinzo Kobori
Senior Vice-President, C. Itoh & Co. (America) Inc.

Peter Karl Kresl
Associate Professor of Economics, Bucknell University, and President, Association for Canadian Studies in the United States

Denis Lamb
Deputy Assistant Secretary for Trade and Commercial Affairs,
U.S. Department of State

Lansing Lamont
Director, Canadian Affairs, Americas Society

Herbert H. Lank
Honorary Director, Du Pont Canada Inc.

Sperry Lea
Vice-President, National Planning Association

Kenneth W. Leeson
Office of the Coordinator for International Communications and Information
Policy, U.S. Department of State

Joseph LeMay
Professor of Political Science, Center for Public Policy Research,
Ramapo College of New Jersey

Edmond A. Lemieux
Executive Vice-President, Finance, Foothills Pipelines (Yukon) Ltd.

David Leyton-Brown
Associate Professor of Political Science, York University

Robert G. Logan
Director, External Programs, IBM Canada Ltd.

Norman T. London
Academic Relations Officer, Canadian Embassy

Robert M. MacIntosh
President, The Canadian Bankers Association

Bruce K. MacLaury
President, The Brookings Institution

Robert L. McNeill
Executive Vice-Chairman, Emergency Committee for American Trade

Robert F. Mathieson
Division Manager, Industries Matters, AT&T

Roy A. Matthews
Economic Council of Canada

James M. Medas
Deputy Assistant Secretary for Canadian Affairs, U.S. Department of State

Allan I. Mendelowitz
Associate Director, U.S. General Accounting Office

William S. Merkin
Deputy Assistant U.S. Trade Representative for the Americas

Myron M. Miller
Vice-President, Business Development, North America,
Sears World Trade, Inc.

Morris Miller
Executive Director, Canada, The World Bank

James P. Monaghan
Vice-President, Alcan Aluminum Corporation

Robert J. Montgomery
Deputy Director, Office of Canadian Affairs, U.S. Department of State

Peter Morici
Vice-President, National Planning Association

Juliet O'Neill
The Canadian Press

Charles Perrault
President, Perconsult Ltd.

Sidney Picker, Jr.
Professor of Law and Chairman, Institute Advisory Board, Canada-United States Law Institute and Case Western Reserve School of Law

Michael Posner
Bureau Chief, Maclean's

Rafael Pozas
Secretary of Economic Affairs, Embassy of Mexico

Ernest H. Preeg
Visiting Fellow, Overseas Development Council

Pierre-Paul Proulx
Senior Economic Advisor, Canadian Department of Regional Industrial Expansion

Myer Rashish
Former Under Secretary of State for Economic Affairs, United States

John W. Reifenberg
Professor, Detroit College of Law

Alfred Reifman
Senior Specialist in International Economics, Congressional Research Service

S. S. Reisman
Former Deputy Minister of Finance, Canada

Richard R. Rivers
Partner, Akin, Gump, Strauss, Hauer and Feld

Berel N.D. Rodal
Director General, Policy Secretariat, Canadian Department of National Defense

Jon Rosenbaum
Assistant U.S. Trade Representative for the Americas

John H. Rouse
Deputy Chief of Mission, U.S. Embassy, Ottawa

Hobart Rowen
Associate Editor, Economics, The Washington Post

Jacques S. Roy
Deputy Chief of Mission and Minister (Economic), Canadian Embassy

Andrew Samet
Associate, Chapman, Duff and Paul

Kenichiro Sasae
First Secretary, Embassy of Japan

J. Robert Schaetzel
Former U.S. Ambassador to the European Community

James Schlesinger
Former Secretary of Energy, United States

Mitchell Sharp
Former Minister of External Affairs, Canada

Horace E. Sheldon
Director, Governmental Affairs Office, Ford Motor Company

David Silversmith
Union College

Irving Sirken
Division Chief, The World Bank

Kenneth S. Smith
World Business Editor, U.S. News & World Report

Joel J. Sokolsky
*Instructor, Canadian Studies, School of Advanced International Studies,
The Johns Hopkins University*

Robert D. Spencer
*Subcommittee on Energy Conservation and Power, U.S. House
of Representatives*

Robert M. Stern
*Professor of Economics and Public Policy, Institute of Public Policy Studies,
University of Michigan*

Maurice F. Strong
Chairman, Canada Development Investment Corporation

Max I. Stucker
Partner, Arthur Andersen & Co.

K. H. Sullivan
*Senior Vice-President, Marketing and Product Support, Pratt & Whitney
Canada*

Alexander C. Tomlinson
President, National Planning Association

Peter M. Towe
Chairman, Petro-Canada International Assistance Corporation

Philip H. Trezise
Senior Fellow, The Brookings Institution

Sandy Vogelgesang
Economic Counselor, United States Embassy, Ottawa, Canada

Jack H. Warren
Vice-Chairman, Bank of Montreal

E. Allan Wendt
*Deputy Assistant Secretary for International Energy and Resources Policy,
U.S. Department of State*

Othol P. White
Vice-President, Government and Public Affairs, Northern Natural Gas Company

William W. Wilson
President, Bank of America Canada

Paul Wonnacott
Professor of Economics, University of Maryland

George W. Woods
Vice-Chairman, TransCanada Pipelines

Gerald Wright
Vice-President, Donner Canadian Foundation